Punk Miracle!?

The Outrageous History of the Sydney Punk Scene 1976-1983

Johnny Rejex

Copyright © 2024 (Johnny Rejex)
All rights reserved worldwide.

No part of the book may be copied or changed in any format, sold, or used in a way other than what is outlined in this book, under any circumstances, without the prior written permission of the publisher.

Prepublication Data Service
P.O. Box 159, Calwell, ACT Australia 2905
Email: publishaspg@gmail.com
http://www.inspiringpublishers.com

 A catalogue record for this book is available from the National Library of Australia

National Library of Australia The Prepublication Data Service

Author: Johnny Rejex
Title: Punk Miracle!?
        The Outrageous History of the Sydney Punk Scene 1976-1983
Genre: Nonfiction

Paperback ISBN: 978-1-923250-23-9

FOREWORD

Punk Rock in Sydney in the seventies was like a riot on a roller coaster. This is not another boring story about bands. This is the story of the crazy characters that stirred the pot of punk pandemonium and helped transform Sydney from a quiet conservative town into the multi-coloured cultural cauldron that it is today. Battles with bikers, combat with cops, street fights with studs and skirmishes with skinheads. It is the story of punk parties where whole houses were destroyed and legends were made. It also tells the tale of an amazing miracle that made me realise that the Sydney scene was blessed whether we liked it or not. In the end it is my memories of all of the mischief and the mayhem but it is probably best to begin at the beginning.

Punk started for me in the library of Fort Street High School sometime in nineteen seventy-six. Surfies were circling like sharks around a boy named Craig Jones. Craig sat listening to something on a set of headphones seemingly unaware of their predatory nature. I didn't like the surfies because they bullied me in tech drawing by insisting that they wanted to have sex with my sister. I didn't like Craig either because he posed as a neo-Nazi and I am prejudiced against racists. The surfies started passing the headphones back and forth whilst mocking Craig's musical taste. I went over to join the circling surfies and took the headphones preparing to join in the chorus of criticism. Proving that you can be both bully and bullied, depending on the circumstances, life can be funny like that!

The sound of Anarchy in the U.K by the Sex Pistols blared into my brain. It was like a Soto mind trick when everything suddenly makes sense because you understand that nothing does. The sound had created a void into which all serious consideration crumbled. I was born again! Redefined by something mysterious, magical and miraculous. The music told me that there was a party going on and that I was invited. Craig and I became fast friends. It turned out that he wasn't a Nazi he just liked the uniforms. We spent weekends together playing world war two board games while listening to punk records. We were on a quest and visited White Light Records in the city to examine the New Musical Express and Melody Maker for anything and everything to do with Punk. At night we would scour the streets armed with spray cans decorating any spare surface with punk propaganda. We spray-painted swastikas on R.S.L Clubs, Punk rules on schools and smiley faces on all the spherical lighting fixtures that adorned the streets of Chatswood.

Chatswood is an upper middle-class suburb on Sydney's north shore. It was like an alien planet to me as I had grown up in Wentworthville in the working-class heart of the western suburbs. I would wait for Craig at Chatswood station amazed by the sight of women wearing makeup to go shopping on Saturday mornings. My mother did not wear makeup except for occasional red lipstick on special occasions. The scent of perfumed affluence was as foreign to me as the Punk dream that I was chasing. Sydney was a very conservative town in the seventies and Chatswood was the capital of conformity. The hippie revolution had barely and belatedly washed up on Sydney's shores much diluted from its journey across the Pacific. There were isolated pockets of long-haired freaks but they were rarely seen and never heard or heeded.

There was still a pub on every city street corner and the smell of a small country town had not yet been overwhelmed by the contemporary sense of sophistication. Every building seemed to have a crane perched upon its roof dragging the city into the sky and somewhat reluctantly into the future. The city centre was all business in the seventies and only came to life in the daytime. It was a working wasteland where no one actually lived. People clung to its fringes like the population of the country clung to the coast.

Despite the seeming calm surface of Sydney society there was always turbulence just below the surface. Most of this underground activity centered around Kings Cross, with various witches and other assorted weirdos circling the streets largely unremarked and unmolested. This was before the train station was built and the Cross was a difficult place to get to. Before there was Punk in Sydney there was also an underground musical movement based on the American alternative scene of the late sixties and early seventies that included bands like MC5, The New York Dolls and of course the Stooges. In Sydney bands such as The Hellcats, Radio Birdman and Black Runner played at a place called the Funhouse above the Oxford Hotel at Taylor Square. I had made plans to go there one night with Craig and another kid from school named Scotch Jim. We were supposed to meet at Museum Station but they never showed up. Expeditions like this were fun with friends but scary for a lone fifteen-year-old boy fresh from the suburbs. I walked up and down Oxford Street and practically wore out the footpath opposite the Oxford Hotel before generating enough courage to cross the road. There was a big hairy guy standing near the door so I asked him who was playing in my best too cool to care voice. He laughed and told me that the venue had closed down the week before.

A few weeks later the three of us did meet at Museum Station and went to see Radio Birdman at Paddington Town Hall. They were loud and thrashy but lacked the irreverent sense of humour that marked the new punk culture. Before they played, we sat in the middle of the floor eating roast chicken and throwing the bones into the crowd along with our disdain. When Birdman finally did play, they generated such contagious energy that we were soon caught up in the excitement and pumped our fists in the air screaming 'yeah hup' along with everybody else. We still had long hair so the only difference between us and them was subtle, philosophical and invisible. We were seeking something that assaulted the altars on which such messianic musicians were worshiped. Birdman were busy becoming messianic and to prove this some members later formed a band called the New Christs. They wanted to be inner city icons and we were busy becoming iconoclasts. Punk has come to be a generic term for all alternative music marked by excessive distortion. If this were true then Link Wray would be the real godfather of punk and not Iggy Pop. In the mid-seventies the term punk related specifically to the English musical movement started by Malcom McLaren and the Sex Pistols. Bands that were aligned with the American scene hated the term and actively opposed the emerging movement. I must admit that when I look at today's bands with their awkward facial hair and sad suburban fashions, I miss Birdman. They were certainly the coolest looking band that Sydney ever saw but if you had called them punk in the late seventies Rob Younger really would have punched you out!

There were a number of bands that arrived on the scene in the seventies that bordered on Punk territory without ever crossing the threshold. Peter Wells, the legendary guitarist from Rose Tattoo, talked about Punk in an interview he did with Lucy De Soto shortly before he died. He said that he had formed the band because he saw nothing in the musical culture at the time that appealed to his taste. Pete could smell Punk on the breeze, like the coming of a storm, but he was already an established musician. He had played bass with the rock band Buffalo in the early seventies. Mick Cox, Angry Anderson and Ian Riland were in the same boat. They were professional musicians looking for work rather than rebels looking for a cause. Ian later left the band and formed X who were the best underground band that Australia ever produced. They played in punk venues and were supported by punks but always had a distinctive style that set them apart from both the mainstream and the emerging punk culture. Both bands were mistakenly described as punk by the press at various times because of their look and attitude but like the Angels and even AC DC they were infected by the Zeitgeist but never really caught the disease.

The thing that I most admire about these bands is that while we were influenced by and the English scene and bands like Birdman had a distinctive American style Rose Tattoo were busy fashioning music with a purely Australian accent. I had a conversation with Ian Riland in the seventies at a flat on Victoria Street in Kings Cross owned by a French woman named Joel in which I discussed my desire to be more Australian. I told him that I had written a song called Drowning which was all about the Sydney scene being flooded by overseas influence. Ian looked at me like I was an idiot but this may have been because I had sneezed rather than snorted over a line of cocaine earlier in the evening. The adulation and success that Rose Tattoo and AC/DC received overseas testifies to the strength of the Australian music scene at the time. The measure of punk success in the Sydney scene is that no one has ever heard of us.

Until the arrival of Punk the city was a wasteland with no discernible youth culture. There was not the abundance of affluent young things that now litter the streets of Newtown and Glebe. The city was exclusively for suits and weekend sightseers when we wandered into town. It must also be remembered that Sharpie gangs had dominated Sydney during the early seventies. From Annandale to Paddington groups of malicious young men with mullets and steel capped boots held sway over Sydney's streets. There were sharpie gangs out in the suburbs too but none of them were as notorious as the Town Hall Sharps. I remember getting off the train at Town Hall station to go to the pictures in George Street fearing the violent confrontation that never eventuated. The Sharpie gangs were territorial and comprised of local youths while punks migrated from all over the country just to be a part of the scene. It was a bit of a miracle that the Sharpie culture disappeared from Sydney's streets when it did or Punk may never have arrived at all.

CHAPTER 1

Punk finally did arrive at the Grand Hotel on Broadway just opposite the bus terminal near Central Station. The Grand Hotel had a lounge bar on the left where regulars and residents of the upstairs flats drank and a public bar on the right which was populated by transient commuters. A hallway ran between these two separate worlds from George Street to a T intersection at the back. To the left was a small room with pool tables and pinball machines. To the right was a bigger room that had obviously been tacked on to the building to host birthday parties and other festive functions. This room became home to the Punk Rock Movement in Sydney. It was a freestanding shed with pathways down both sides that led to the toilets out the back. The room was entered through double glass doors and had a long bar running up the right-hand side. There was also a toilet at the back of the room behind where the bands played. The sight of punters crossing this hitherto holy sanctuary in order to urinate was inspiring in itself. There was no actual stage at the Grand Hotel which suited the new punk ethos perfectly as it placed everyone on the same level whether they liked it or not. The licensee of the Grand Hotel was a hard little bloke named Dennis who didn't mind getting personally involved when trouble started. A knockabout bloke named Fred managed the pub. Fred was everybody's friend and was on a first name basis with all of the regulars. He had a habit of rewarding his favourites with a free yard glass on their eighteenth birthday which seemed to happen several times for some. He was a hardheaded man with a heart of gold and somehow managed to stay calm even when there was a riot erupting all around him.

We had been drawn to the venue by advertisements for a band called Johnny Dole and the Scabs and it was Johnny Dole that greeted us at the door. He was a lanky looking Pom with long hair and leathers and a cheeky grin that invited you in. You paid two dollars at the door and got a raffle ticket for a bottle of cheap Champaign. Johnny would always rig the raffle and we would always win. He did it because we were poor and because he needed our support but mostly because he was mischievous by nature. I almost got into a fight with Johnny a short time later when he hit a friend of mine over the head with a microphone stand. I was so upset that I waited for him in the back alleyway after the gig without really considering the consequences. Johnny soon appeared out of the back door with a broken bottle in his hand. I wrapped my coat around my arm as I had seen people do in knife fights in the movies. I told him to put down the bottle and he told me to put down the coat. I told him to fight like a man and he told me to fight like a punk. The whole situation was becoming absurd when his band backed a car up the alley at dangerous speed. Johnny jumped in and they sped off like the cops were chasing them. For years afterwards Johnny would remind me of how green I was and how he had taught me the difference between a clean fight and a street fight.

The Scabs did not look like a punk band at all. They had long hair and wore flared jeans but so did everyone else back then. They played a variety of covers from the sixties and seventies with a few originals thrown in. They were so distorted that they certainly sounded punk. Their most popular song was 'I don't wanna work' which was a hook that the crowd could chant like an anthem while pumping their fists in the air. In retrospect it was all probably just a marketing ploy in order to cash in on the publicity that the British punk scene had been receiving in the main stream media. Johnny was a shameless self-promoter which was just as well or the Sydney punk scene might never have started at all. One night he did a radio interview in one of the rooms upstairs. We went up to see what was happening and he let me speak. I said something so stupid that I have decided to deny that I said anything at all. He later talked some current affair program into filming one of their gigs. That night the back room was packed with posing Paddington trendies all pogoing for position in front of the cameras. The television story climaxed with a shot of Johnny breaking a fake bottle over his own head. This seemed lame considering how many real bottles got broken over other heads at other times but we didn't care because we were there and there was magic in the air.

The other regular bands at the Grand Hotel were Tommy and the Dipsticks, Rocks and Black Runner. Tommy and the Dipsticks were refugees from garages in the southern suburbs and were willing to play to anyone who was willing to listen. They looked like the Beatles but played more like the Stones and would never really escape the sixties. Rocks were a three piece with a singing drummer who called himself Bill Posters. For those who don't know posters used to be called bills and people who put them up were called posters. There were signs everywhere in the city saying that bill posters would be prosecuted. Rocks were the only underground band with a record at the time. It was an E.P was entitled 'You're so Boring'. They played fast and furious and are apparently still playing this way at venues around the city in some form today. Other bands like Voigt 465, X L Capris and even Mental as Anything played at the Grand Hotel at various times but the Dipsticks and Rocks were regulars and integral to the scene starting.

The other band integral to the start of the scene and central to its continued existence was Black Runner. The first night that I saw Black Runner play I was convinced that the singer was an evil dwarf. The singer was Jimmy Bedhog but he wasn't called that yet because the Bedhogs hadn't happened. He later proved that he was evil by stabbing some punter in the back with a broken flagon but turned out to be of relatively normal size. He was built like a bandy-legged bull terrier and he had a personality to match. One moment he would be playing like a puppy and the next he would be biting off your ear. He had a nose that had been broken so often that his head had twisted around it out of sympathy. He looked that way because he had been thrown through the windscreen of a car when he was a kid. He attracted and repelled at the same time with equal force and exuded chaos and charisma in like measure. Jimmy suggested such contradictions but he also lived them. He was probably the perfect punk except punk was far from perfect.

The guitar player in Black Runner was Jimmy's older brother Danny Rumour. Both boys were from a town called Bargo just south of Sydney. Danny had grown up in the city with his grandparents. He had attended Cleveland Street Boys High School. This was the hardest High School in the city. When there was trouble at Cleveland Street High School, they didn't call for the cane they called for the Dog Squad. Danny had straight shoulders and always stood square to the ground. He had bright blue eyes, jet-black hair and the requisite seventies sideburns. He looked like rock n' roll and sounded like it too. He could play the Stooges with all the requisite raw power but could also pick a Gene Vincent cover with perfect precision. He was the gun guitar player in the scene and later proved to be the best in the country with his licks in The Cruel Sea.

It would be fair to say that Danny started the Punk scene in Sydney with Black Runner and finished it off with Sekret Sekret. It would also be fair to say this of Peter Perfect who played guitar in the

Scabs and also played in Sekret Sekret. But it would be fairer to say that Jimmy started the punk scene in Sydney with Black runner, perfected it with the Bedhogs and finished it off with the Kelpies, who nowadays refer to themselves as a post-punk band. Danny played with the Urban Guerillas and the Bedhogs but he was never a punk. He was part of the old school Funhouse crowd who wanted to be considered cool and counted us as clowns. He derided the new English fashion to me at the Grand Hotel one night. I wanted to object but Danny was just too cool to contradict. Jimmy embraced the outrageousness of the new movement as it suited his personality perfectly. It was not long before he traded basic black for the multi-coloured madness that was the punk scene in Sydney.

CHAPTER 2

The only other venue with punk pretensions at the time was Blondies at Bondi Junction. Blondies was upstairs in a solid sandstone building that looked like it had been a bank and attracted the same sort of crowd. You entered through a foyer with a floor of smooth black and white tiles that looked like marble but were probably just polished stone. You then went up a cold stone staircase with an ornate metal balustrade. You felt like you were entering a palace which made you feel even more like a pauper. Borderline punk acts like Crime and the City Solution and the Particles played there but they seemed more interested in establishing themselves rather than establishing a scene. The crowd at Blondies was more up market than the one at the Grand Hotel. Although the eastern suburbs were not as conservative as those on the north shore there was just as much money there. Punk culture did not automatically exclude rich kids but when you are already on top of the world you are not really interested in turning it upside down.

We mainly went to Blondies in order to please Vonnie. Craig and I met Vonnie on the Manly ferry on our way home from snorkeling at Fairy bower beach. She looked like a sea nymph who had scrambled aboard in order to amuse herself amongst the mere mortals. She was short with matching short, spiked blonde hair. She had beautiful hazel eyes that sparkled with mischief. She kept staring at my Sex Pistols T-shirt before disappearing mysteriously back into the crowd. I couldn't catch her but eventually she caught me as witches will. She told me that she wanted to be a punk so I told her about the Grand Hotel. She asked me for a lock of my hair so that she could put a spell on me. I gave to her freely because I wanted to be under her spell. She later magically appeared at the Grand Hotel on the same night as the television cameras. She was wonderfully wicked but innocent at heart which was the very soul of the punk scene in Sydney.

The other major punk venue started sometime in 1977 when a band named World War Four appeared at the Grand Hotel. They had a front man with a crewcut called Bruce. He distributed business cards advertising a punk club called The Last Resort. The club was upstairs through a non-descript doorway in the alleyway just behind the Oxford hotel on Taylors Square. It was a large room that looked like it had been used as a storage space for a long time. It had dirty fibro walls and dusty wooden floors with a makeshift stage at the far end. The Last Resort promised but did not ultimately provide the place that we were seeking. X, Johnny Dole and the Scabs and World War Four played there often but the scene was the same. The venue was actually a hard-core queer nightclub called Sids that had given Bruce Friday nights for punk performances. We found this out by turning up on a Saturday night and finding ourselves surrounded by drag queens. We weren't homophobic but the hard-core queer scene in Sydney in the seventies could be terrifying. The most popular queer venue at that time was Patches on Oxford Street. There weren't any gay nightclubs at the time because the term had not been invented yet.

We used to go to Patches for late night drinks sometimes because Sydney was still suffering from ten o'clock closing. I went to Patches with Jimmy Bedhog and some friends one night. We took a corner table near the stage and played about like punks until the show started. A drag queen then took the stage and started stripping. The performer was use to intimidating the audience and decided to target us because we looked young and unaccustomed. Jimmy responded by barking like a dog and mounting the stage on all fours. The drag queen sensibly backed away but Jimmy wasn't shy and followed the performer across the stage aiming his snapping teeth at a half-exposed crotch. The drag queen backed up too fast and staggered right off the edge of the stage onto a table spilling drinks and drunks everywhere. We were bounced straight away but at least we went out laughing.

Meanwhile back at the Last Resort the guy who greeted us at the door was a tattooed ex-con named Tony. He was very tough and very queer which was very weird. The only queer men I had seen had been winsome cynical souls in British comedies. The club didn't have a liquor license so Scotch Jim would get Bruce to go to the Oxford Hotel and buy us a carton. Jim had left school at the end of fourth form and was working as an apprentice. The beer bought friends including Mad Dog. He was the head of the Hurstville boys and the son of the head biker from the Ghost Riders. He was short and stocky with a long ponytail. He walked with a swagger that insinuated violence and matched his persistent snarl. His best mate was Animal who was as tall as Mad Dog was short. He had curly black hair, long lavish sideburns and bushy black beard to match. They were both named Dave so they needed the nicknames and deserved them as well.

The other person we met on our first night at The Last Resort was a skinny kid who was a few years older than us called Les Wreckage. Les had floppy black hair, false teeth and an infectious sense of humour. He had a personality that was like a champagne cork popping even though he spent most of the time trying to get back in the bottle. He was a Catholic country boy who had been sent to boarding school and had the psychological scars to prove it. He was the first person that I ever saw who looked and acted like a punk. He came all the way from Moulmein near Hay to stagger up to our table at the Last Resort and set himself on fire. Craig leapt from his chair and put him out with cold beer only to be told off by Les for wasting good beer. Les was the personification of punk in Sydney. He became the philosophical guru and the undisputed arbiter of fashion and music as the movement moved forward.

The other person of note who was attracted by our beer was Nick Sleaze. He was a fellow cultural refugee from the western suburbs of Sydney and hailed from Scotch Jim's hometown of Mount Druitt. Nick was the son of European refugees who had traveled to Australia via London and he still carried a slight English accent. He had dirty brown hair that snaked around the collar of his blue-collar clothes. He had bad skin and worse fashion sense but he was very smart and later became the bass player in Rejex. Along with the Hurstville boys we formed a tight crew. We were setting sail for parts unknown searching for a secret treasure. No one knew where we were going but we felt that the wind was at our backs and our punk paradise was somewhere not too far in our future.

Inspired by Les' flaming fashion show I started making my own punk clothes on my mother's old Singer sewing machine. Cutting up old black pants and duffle coats, sewing on zippers and making epaulets from sections of a studded brown belt. I took in the legs of all my jeans to make stovepipes and added as many safety pins as I could steal. I also found a pair of boots at the Merrylands Mall that looked like brothel creepers, even though I didn't know what brothel creepers were at the time. They had huge rubber soles and even bigger buckles and were the closest thing I could find to the photos in NME. Carmel Streamline did have a punk clothes shop in Paddington at the time but purchasing punk clothes was anathema to real punks and you would only wear them if you wanted to become a spit magnet.

When I finally emerged in my newly made punk clothes people avoided me like the plague. I cleared the carriage when I got on the train at Wentworthville and headed into town. I was wearing bright red jeans with big black zippers, a ripped T-shirt and an army surplus jacket died black and covered in safety pins. The only person who didn't seem terrified was an old lady who sat down next to me and asked if I was going out dancing. She then raved on about how much she had loved to dance when she was young and we talked all the way into town. Her attitude seemed stranger than my clothes at the time. I realised later that people of her generation had already witnessed two world wars and a great depression so they were probably going to be pretty hard to shock.

I waited for Craig and Scotch Jim to arrive at Museum Station and was surprised when they were more terrified of my look than the passengers on the train. Even though they were sympathetically dressed in black they insisted on walking ten yards behind me all the way up to the Rex Hotel in Kings Cross. We had made it all the way up William Street and half way down Darlinghurst Road before the Bikers outside the tattoo parlour decided to call my bluff and one of them called out, 'look it's the girl guides.' It was an accurate critique delivered with immaculate timing. We ended up laughing all the way to the pub.

The Rex Hotel was on Darlinghurst road just down past the fountain. The downstairs bar was called the bottoms up bar and was as queer as the name suggested. On this particular night a couple of strays had wandered upstairs to check out the talent. They were coming in to the toilet as I was going out and might have been cruising but I didn't take much notice. When I got back to the bar Mad Dog came up to ask me what had happened. I wasn't sure what he meant. He then stormed into the toilet with Betty to find out for himself. Betty was an iron bar about six inches long that Mad Dog carried around in his back pocket. He may have felt offended by what he assumed was their predatory nature. He may have been behaving like my big brother or perhaps he just felt like a fight. I didn't go in after him because I didn't know what he was doing. I did feel sad for the two queens who were left bleeding on the toilet floor purely because Mad Dog was mad.

The madness of Mad Dog was perfectly illustrated when we went to a party at his house in Hurstville sometime later that year. The house was an ordinary suburban fibro shack except that it was decorated with motorcycle parts. The first order of business was to go into the garage and taste his dad's homemade slivovitz. It was taken in a small shot glass for a reason. Mad Dog liked to mix it with red cordial in a large glass in order to entice the unwary drinker into oblivion. He also used the cordial to get his young cousins to take a taste and found it highly amusing when they started to throw up all over the backyard. This was pretty shocking at the time because these kids were only around five years old.

The only rule at Mad Dog's house was that everyone had to piss on the first person to crash out. You have to be pretty pissed to piss on someone but we were all suitably primed when John Moron succumbed to the slivovitz later in the evening. He wasn't happy when he realized that he had lost the game and grabbed a knife from a table in order to demonstrate his displeasure. Mad Dog walked slowly towards him while telling him very calmly that no one pulled a knife at his house. John had seemed quite frightening but now seemed only frightened. He backed away towards the fence as Mad Dog approached. John raised the knife at the last moment but Mad Dog punched him over the wire fence and into the next yard before he had a chance to use it. He then lent over the prostrate Moron and took the knife from him telling him that he could only return to the party if he apologised. Only Mad Dog could make a knife-wielding maniac seem so lame.

Later in the evening some of the Ghost Riders appeared and immediately began selecting which boys they would rape. I don't believe they were serious unless they were so pissed that they really thought that we were the girl guides. I don't know what happened to Mad Dog and Betty on this occasion. The only one to stand up to them was Animal who challenged them to a game of tackle football out on the bitumen road. As animal was being crashed tackled onto the asphalt the rest of us started jumping fences. We hid in backyards and shuffled through the shadows until we eventually found our way back to the railway station and went home suitably shaken.

CHAPTER 3

The Grand Hotel closed for a while at this time, whatever time this was, and the Last Resort didn't last long. The promise of a punk paradise remained unfulfilled. For a while it seemed that the Punk scene in Sydney would die before it even got started. We spent our exile drinking and listening to Les' considerable punk record collection. This all happened in his caravan which was parked in his uncle's driveway in Seven Hills. I don't know how we all fitted into that van or how his uncle put up with the noise. I do remember that we had to drag the caravan back up to the house every morning as it had danced down the driveway during the night. It was during one of these evenings that Les played an E.P by a Sydney band called the Thought Criminals. It didn't have great production values but it was pretty funny. We soon located them in the gig guide at the Native Rose in Chippendale and our exile came to an end.

The Thought Criminals were a bunch of Private School kids who had obviously taken their inspiration from George Orwell's 1984. They had a really good guitar player named Steve who looked straight but played crazy and later had some mainstream success with the bass player from Friction in a band called Do Re Mi. The singer was a short guy named Bruce whose spiked blonde hair was almost taller than he was. He looked like a dirty old man because he always had his hands in the pockets of a dirty old overcoat. He didn't have a great voice but he did have a great pair of sunglasses that lit up in red. He would employ them along with various other mechanical devices in a kind of cabaret performance that would have gone down really well in Melbourne. They were fast and poppy were a really good dance band because they had a really good drummer. They say that you know a really good drummer because you don't notice them. This guy was so good that I can't even remember his name. The bass player always wore a suit which was comically ironic when they performed No, No, No, No, Mr. Suit by Wire. His name was Roger and he would later form a record label called Double Think. He would start this business by recording singles for Rejex and Suicide Squad and later went on to run Festival records Australia. Roger never sold out because he was born in a suit. He was never really a punk but he will always be a thought criminal. We were just happy to be back in town and part of a scene even if it was in a cold concrete beer garden at the back of the pub. Fortunately the Grand Hotel opened up again shortly after this and punk proper was about to take its first few faltering footsteps.

The main bands during this second coming were The Urban Guerillas, The Broken Toys and last but not least The Last Words. The guitar player from the Urban Guerillas was called Short Bob. He had his name around backwards because he was very tall and very thin. He had a long-hooked nose, shaggy dark hair and dark brown eyes that intimated mischief. He projected a maniacal presence that perfectly suited his punk performances. The first time that I saw the legendary guitar player from the Urban Guerillas he was in a band called Filth who were playing at a party. The party was filled with Funhouse veterans and I don't remember much about it. We only went because a family friend of Craig's was singing in the band. The second time that I saw Bob he was perched over the back door of the band room at the Grand Hotel like he was levitating. Hovering over the room like a living gargoyle. He is still playing around Sydney in The Light Brigade.

Bob had told the rest of the band never to smile on stage. This proved to be impossible for the singer Andy who was the sole female performer at the time. Andy was a short girl with a big voice and had a smile that could light up the room. She would wear pink leopard skin tights and crazy coloured spiked hair that changed colour almost as often as she changed clothes. Ross had been Andy's high school sweetheart when they were young and in Glen Innes and played the bass. Ross was tall, dark and lean with short-cropped black hair and a hand grenade tattooed on his upper arm. He had a weird way of sucking in his cheeks and pursing his lips when he played. It made it seem like he was either whistling while he worked or he wanted to kiss the world because he was having so much fun. They went through a number of drummers but the first I remember was Coz. He was a curly headed blonde kid who was always very cool but who took his cool to the cold streets of London far too soon. The Urban Guerillas were the one band that managed to bridge the divide between the American and English scenes. They had their roots firmly planted in the soil of American music but their sense of style was imported directly from England. They played the Stooges and Mc5 while writing originals that reflected the new mood. "Smash Your T.V. was the most memorable of these songs because of its anthem like chorus. They were a great band!

The Broken Toys were three young boys from Sydney's southern suburbs. The guitar player was a tall kid named Andrew who had long black spikes for hair. He had clean skin, long limbs and a really good, high pitched voice. David Virgin played the bass and was Andrew's physical opposite. He had short, spiked blonde hair, pale blue eyes and low-pitched voice. He was from a large family of Irish immigrants and still suffered from a Gaelic lilt. David's younger brother John Boy played the drums but had to hand over the sticks to Coz when Fred found out that he was only thirteen. They had a great pop sensibility and harmonised well. David was certain that he was going to be a star. When I told him how good they were he told people that I was his fan. I took to pinching his cheeks and ruffling his hair every time that I saw him to dispel such silliness. If the Broken Toys had happened anywhere else in the world David's dreams may have come true. In the Sydney punk scene such sentiments inevitably led to nightmares.

The Last Words were the closest thing to stars that the Sydney punk scene had seen. They had recently returned from England where they had put out a single entitled Animal World. They were the first band that I saw play at the Grand Hotel with a full PA system and a light show. They carried a sense of celebrity because of their recent proximity to the holy sites and personages of the punk scene in London and like stars they kept their distance. The singer was a short stocky guy with very short hair named Malcolm. He had bad acne scars and a great raspy voice as if the scars had made their way right through to his vocal chords. The bass player was a social animal named Lee who was the first person that I met with an abiding love of reggae. He was long and lean with matching long black spiked hair that always seemed to be drunk because it could never stand up straight. The guitar player had the golden curls of a cherub but played like a demon and called himself Andy Groom. He seemed too serious to be a punk and like Malcolm he was rarely seen in public when he was not playing. John Gunn played drums and was one of the best skin men to play in the scene. He later played with the Urban Guerillas when Coz went on his pilgrimage to London. Their most memorable gig was on the footpath outside of the pictures on George Street when the *Rock n' Roll Swindle* movie was released. Everyone felt betrayed by Malcolm McLaren's version of events. The gig by The Last Words turned out to be better than the movie. It took several years for Johnny Rotten's side of the story to be heard in *The Filth and the Fury* but the wait was worth the feeling of vindication. Johnny Rotten was the undisputed king of punk to anyone who knew anything which was hardly anybody at the time.

The new lease of life for the Grand and the new bands brought a whole new group of people to the scene including Kirsty, who had the same last name as me and went on to edit a main stream fashion magazine. Robyn, the sister of Slim Jim, who later played drums with Sekret Sekret and the Cruel Sea and Jenny who wore a permanent smile and is still good friends with the Guerillas. They were all good-looking girls who shared a natural teenage enthusiasm for fun and music and improved the mood as well as the look of the scene. There was also Dancing Dez, who was an Asian looking guy with long black spikey hair and immaculate fashion sense. He could take the focus of the audience away from the band by simply standing near the stage and acting like he had something to say. Dez would walk up the pathway outside of the band room and strike a pose in each of the windows that ran along the sides of the building. It would not take long until the whole room would be watching him instead of the band. He developed a unique dancing style which was later copied by several punks. It involved pumping his arms up and down directly in front of him while moving his feet wildly in every direction as if he was forever almost falling over. Dez personified the idea of Punk being all about performance. The bands were only a distraction from the main stage which was everybody else in the room.

The punk scene was a family affair in Sydney and there were many sets of brothers. Besides Jim and Danny and Andy and Des and David and John Boy there was a long-haired guy named Tom who saw the Scabs and was followed by his younger brother Peer who entered the scene at Thirteen and is still hanging around like punk perfume. There was also the Greek boys Chris and Manny who were like Chinese dolls, Chris being the bigger and Manny the older. They cornered the market in Beta porn just before the world went VHS but later made a killing playing paintball at Heartbreak Ridge. There were also the Porters, the Crastis and the Knuckle brothers. The Knuckles would later form the Wet

Taxis in the mid-eighties with a guy named Louis Toilet. Louis never talked to anyone and slunk around the shadows in a green army jacket with 'death lives' on the back. He would occasionally tickle the ivories on the old upright piano in the corner of the band room. Tim Knuckle still plays in bands like Satellite 5 with Paul Hayward from the Baddies and the Flipped-Out Kicks with Johnny Gretsch from the Wasted Ones.

There were also a couple of fifteen-year-old kids named Rod Rodent and Chris Cross who would form the core of the social scene for many years to come. Rod had grown up rough in the TNT towers at Redfern. He shared a heritage with Chris Cross of having holidays in a boy's homes. Rod was tall and thin with dark hair and bad skin. He had a crooked mouth to match his words and even though he had a huge nose his eyes were still too close together. Rod received his nickname because he could crawl up your psychological drainpipe and steal your most personal thoughts and your most personal possessions before you even knew that you owned them. He could sniff out an opportunity before it arose and could lie so well that he could even convince himself. He once kicked a wino when we were walking through the city and I was about to tell him off when the wino rolled over and smiled. He called Rod by name and Rod stuck a couple of dollars in the old man's pocket before we moved on. I also remember him standing on the balcony at a party at Joel's place one night with a kitten in his hands. He asked the punk girls present what was the best thing about kittens. The girls cooed and carried on and said that kittens were cuddly and soft and sweet. Rod cuddled the kitten for a second and then told them that the best thing about kittens was that they could land on their feet. He then threw the kitten over the balcony to plummet thirteen floors to the ground below. He was a rodent after all.

Chris Cross was similarly built except that he had blonde hair and green eyes. He was all limbs and laughter and would eat a whole loaf of bread with a block of cheese, a savory sausage and two bottles of beer for a snack. If Jimmy was like a bull terrier then Chris was like big friendly Labrador pup. He could smell someone tripping from three miles away and could lick the brains out of your ear before you had the sense to slap him away. Chris Cross was a rock star long before he ever played in a band. He had several aliases including Christian Priest and had documents to authenticate all of them. He was always a favourite with the ladies. He went on to play bass in the Bedhogs and later flirted around the fringes of fame with the Dropbears.

Cathi Corpse was an undoubted star of the Sydney punk scene. She was tall and lanky with longish, spiked hair. She was really smart and rarely straight. A predilection for downers earned her the nickname Corpse. We wanted her to run for mayor at one time for a political party called 'Punks Against People' with the campaign slogan 'the only good politician is a dead politician.' But she was always too out of it to enter. Cathi later left Sydney and went outback to get fit as a jillaroo. She then moved to the America and travelled around the country with a Native American dance troupe. She married one of the members who was a full blood Arapaho named Soldier Wolf. She has since become a mother and is a martial arts instructor.

Cathi had a pet chook named Chook that she would carry around to gigs. Chook would follow Cathi around like a dog and came whenever she would call. Cathi and Peer and some other punks went to Centennial Park one night and set chook free. Cathi got a tattoo of Chook on her arm. Even though it looked like a cartoon the tattoo represented something more real to Cathi than most people. There were numerous times when some wannabe punk would stand at the bar at the Grand Hotel fascinated by Cathi's tattoo. No matter how great their interest or how persistent their questioning the only response they would ever get was 'Chook'. Chook needed no further explanation. Cathi was so Zen that reality had a hard time keeping up with her. Her Chook tattoo was more punk than most punks.

Cathi was also at the centre of the first Sydney punk scene miracle. After gigs we would gather on the street outside exhausted and covered with sweat. We would then decide collectively what mischief we would indulge in next. On this particular occasion Cathi decided to stop the world. She wandered out onto Broadway with her arms outstretched demanding that the traffic cease and desist. The traffic didn't cease in time and Cathi was hit by a car. She flew through the air and landed hard on the road. We held our collective breathe. Cathi bounced back up and approached the car like a crazed zombie. She leant over the bonnet so that her face was as close to the windscreen as she could get and abused the shocked motorist for several seconds. The motorists' mind must have gone from shock to relief to terror in a few seconds and appeared to be paralysed. When Cathi had finished her diatribe, she walked toward us with her arms in the air celebrating her victory and resurrection. Because she had been hidden by the car the bus driver in the next lane did not see and the bus hit her hard. She soared several metres through the air twisting and tumbling like an acrobat. She hit the ground so hard that there should have been a crater. Everyone on the footpath stood stunned. The bus driver leapt from the bus and approached the prostrate corpse. Before he could reach her Cathi bounded to her feet and after standing shakily for several seconds started to abuse him. He was so terrified that he started running for the bus with Cathi in hot pursuit. He was lucky that the multiple collisions had slowed her down. He managed to clamber onboard and close the doors before she could get him. Cathi pounded on the doors and continued her tirade of abuse until she ran out of steam. She gave the bus driver the finger and rejoined us on the side of the road. Proving that it is impossible to kill a corpse and drugs can almost kill you and save your life all at the same time, drugs can be funny like that!

CHAPTER 4

The punk movement found a house that soon became a home in Stanmore. The original inhabitants of the house were a couple of Kiwi communists called Kevin and Gerard. They distributed political propaganda around the scene. This did not go down well with the prevailing nihilist ethos. Believing in something was totally against everything that we believed. They had a friend named Greg who turned up to the Grand with 'Free Chile' written on his T-shirt. When punks persisted in asking for a plate full it quickly undermined his political determination. He also took to wearing a dog collar which earned him the nickname Greg Dog. He had thick, curly black hair, bushy eyebrows and big lips. He was well built and had a low growl to his voice that also suited his nickname. He did well with the ladies and ended up banging the barmaid from the Grand. I remember seeing him years later at the trendy Stranded Disco surrounded by young punk girls. They would hang around him like a harem until a popular song was played. Then they would go and collect as many drinks as they could from vacant tables when everyone else got up to dance. The best thing about these three people was that they were broke so they were looking for people to move in. Les and Nick took up their offer and they formed the first exclusively punk household. Everyone seemed to live there all the time. Stanmore was only one suburb away from where Craig and I were finishing our high school education so we could get changed and walk over in the afternoons. On weekends I used to interrupt my journey to the city to get off at Stanmore station so we could all ride into town like a gang. This was like a travelling circus. Every public space was seen as a place for punk performance. We were never overly aggressive or violent. Our appearance and posture were overwhelming enough for the average passenger. We were evangelizing our cause but I don't remember ever converting any casual commuters. It was enough that that the scene was being seen.

One night when we arrived at the Grand there was a group of suburban refugees waiting for us. They told us later that they were about to go home disappointed when the circus finally came to town. The chaotic carnival shattered their sense of self and turned them into carefree clowns. They were a group of kids from Chester Hill including Little Stuart who later played guitar in the Bedhogs and later still in the Allnighters. There was also a kid named Frazer who had curly brown hair and what seemed like a permanent tan. He always looked straight no matter how out of it he was. There was a guy named Brian who looked like a cartoon vampire and spent the next few years seriously trying to decide what his nickname would be but never could come to a conclusion. The most prominent personality was Pommy Ian who was a big kid with a big nose and an even bigger appetite for drugs. He later became an infamous pill head and a very good friend of mine. He ended up working as a roadie for INXS before moving back to England. They also had a friend named John the Baptist who earned this nickname because he refused to give up his religious convictions. He sometimes came to gigs dressed in his Boy Scout uniform when his meeting had run late. He was the only punk that persisted in their beliefs despite all the peer pressure that we could bring to bear. He was the most outrageous of all the punks because he was so straight. He was truly a voice crying in the wilderness. They all became full time punk participants and regular guests at the Stanmore house.

One of my favorite stories about Stanmore was when the house was being raided regularly by the police because of burglaries that were happening in the area. Rod Rodent was particularly upset by the constant contact with police. He was innocent on this particular occasion and professional pride made him jealous of the true perpetrators. Rod soon started scouting the surrounding suburb for clues. He made friends with all of the neighbors including some crazy lady named Bubbles who he had sex with for information. He eventually uncovered the criminal gang and discovered that they had escaped police detection by storing the stolen goods in an electrical sub-station across the road. Rod was very impressed by their cunning and told everyone how clever they were before taking them down. He talked a kid named Bailey from Brisbane into lending him his car. Bailey was a serpentine creature with suitably slimy looking skin. He always seemed to be scheming something like some comic book villain. He was a sixteen-year old runaway who had stolen his mother's car to come to Sydney. He wore a long black coat with the pockets ripped out so that he could fill the lining with food at parties. I don't know whether he wore the same coat for several years or had several coats over the years but he always looked the same. Bailey could talk his way into or out of anything and could provide a feast including whole chickens and loaves of bread from the inside of his magic coat at any time of day or night. After borrowing Bailey's station wagon Rod and Chris cased the sub-station until they knew it was full of goodies and then stole the lot. When I recounted the story in front of Rod years later, he denied everything, so I knew that it was true.

The house at Stanmore was also special to me personally for two main reasons. It was the house where Rejex was formed and it was also where I was staying when I was arrested for assault and robbery. The band was formed after a group of us woke up in a strange house one morning extremely hungover. The initial idea was to write songs that anyone could play so that we could invite any member of the movement to learn them and join us on stage. We wanted to reduce the space between the audience and the band to nothing. It was only the fact that none of us could play that allowed this illusion to flourish. When we got back to the house at Stanmore and announced our idea it was met with enthusiasm in principle but not in practice. Greg Dog decided he should be the singer and wasn't willing to share the role so we had a competition. We both wrote a song and let the other members of the band decide who should sing. I remember his song was called 'red roof girl', which was a suburban love song. I can't remember what I wrote but since the whole thing was my idea anyway, he really didn't have a chance.

We rehearsed in Nick's bedroom with the mandatory mattresses blocking the doors and windows. The original lineup consisted of Paul with a car on guitar. Paul was a straight looking guy with short brown hair and a serious disposition who was one of many people that liked to act crazy but didn't see the need to dress that way. Richard also played guitar. He was a university student with curly blonde hair, a hairy chest and a permanent three o'clock shadow. He seemed to be part surfer, part hippie and part rocker. He could play a few David Bowie songs that no one could recognize. Nick Sleaze became the bass player because no one else wanted the role. He couldn't play at all at the time but ended up being the most musically talented. He was also left-handed which made finding an instrument difficult so he ended up playing a right-handed bass upside down.

Despite the early displays of enthusiasm no one else wanted to rehearse and Paul with a car soon dropped out. Richard, Nick and I persisted and soon got a kid named Stuart to play drums. This was good because he had a room under his parent's house where we could rehearse. We were terrible at the time and only persisted because we had nothing better to do and because the punk ethos told that us that we could. Our first gig was at a party that Les held at Stanmore. We had bought a guitar amp and speaker from Peter Perfect. It had Scabs spray painted across the front so it was like a religious relic. We also bought a bass amp and a green speaker box from Ross Guerilla. These artifacts allowed us to see ourselves as the heirs of the original legends and the natural choice to continue the culture. I don't remember much about the party except that I got really drunk and then complained to everyone that they had arrived too late and we were now too drunk to play but we played anyway.

The best thing about this era was that there were now two venues again. We would go to the Grand Hotel to watch whatever band was playing and then travel up Broadway to the Native Rose to see the Thought Criminals. The Grand Hotel closed at ten o'clock as did most hotels at the time. The Native Rose closed at eleven because it served food although I don't remember ever eating there. We did this so regularly that the night watchman at the Tafe used to wait with a cup of coffee to watch us pass by. We would press ourselves against the windows and pogo on the stairs to show that we appreciated his attention. I think we were just happy that someone outside the movement was acknowledging our existence. His fascination demonstrated that Punk had finally arrived in Sydney as a regular and recognisable presence. When we arrived at the Native Rose, we would walk straight through the bar to the beer garden out the back in order to catch the end of the Thought Criminals set.

The only incident of note that happened at the Native Rose involved an outlaw motorcycle club which will remain nameless for my own protection. I was standing in back room after the Thought Criminals had finished when someone ran in and said that there was a fight outside between punks and bikers. This seemed insensible because the majority of punks could not fight. Any conflict involving a biker gang could only end in our complete and utter annihilation. I followed the bearer of the bad news outside and had my suspicions immediately confirmed. There was no mass battle only a group of punks and bikers standing around in a circle watching someone get their head smashed in. I made my way through the crowd and saw Greg Dog lying on the ground with a big hairy biker sitting on his chest. The punks in the crowd stood frozen in fear while the bikers cheered. Fortunately, sirens started blaring in the background which signaled the end of the fight. Unfortunately, the bikers decided that this should signal the end of Greg Dog as well and stood around yelling 'waste him, waste him.' It was only the threat of death that got me involved, otherwise I doubt I would have summoned the courage to do anything. I ran through the circle of onlookers and put my right shoulder into the biker. I knocked him clear which enabled Greg to get to his feet. The other bikers had heeded the sirens and were running for their bikes. I had time to get Greg around the corner and under a parked car before their pursuit started. We lay there for some seconds before the unmistakable rumble of Harley engines drifted around the corner and headed slowly down our street. Greg wanted to get out from under the car and continue the fight but I managed to convince him that this was not a good idea. We waited until the trouble had passed before getting out from under the car. We took Greg to the hospital and found that he had an arm badly broken in several places. Fortunately, fortune doesn't always favour the brave.

Meanwhile, some punks from Canberra had contacted someone from Sydney and asked for a band to come down and play on a big night that they were planning. I don't know how Rejex got the gig but I never knew how we got gigs they seemed to just happen like magic. We drove down in Bailey's station wagon and Paul with a car came too. We packed as many punks as possible into the cars available and headed down the highway blocking both lanes while driving really slowly. This proved to be very annoying for our fellow travelers but it was all part of the performance. We would wait for the people behind us to get totally enraged and start honking and screaming before we would let them pass and bare our bums. This display along with our bizarre appearance tended to quiet them down and speed them on their way.

The gig was in a large old hall somewhere in the suburbs and we drove around endless roundabouts looking for it. Sydney did not have roundabouts at the time and they seemed like an apt metaphor for Canberra's convoluted political culture. We eventually arrived and were told where to set up and to be wary of a guy named Trog. Trog was the local madman and had a very violent reputation. I can't remember anything about the gig or even who else played but I do remember Trog coming up to us at the end of the evening with a broken beer bottle. He hovered aggressively over a couple of the girls whose maternal instincts had been roused when he decided to pick on Peer. I decided to be chivalrous and punched him in the head. He fell to the ground and lay pathetically prostrate. The malicious mothers then mauled him without mercy. Laura Horizontal jumped all over him with her stiletto heels while Cathi Corpse put in the boot. After the frenzy faltered, we found out that it had been Trog who had invited us and that he was also welcoming us into his home. We went back his house to sleep after driving around several roundabouts several times on the way. Trog had a girlfriend and a baby and seemed very mild mannered in his modest home. I remember thinking that while we had to work really hard to make Sydney seem strange people in Canberra didn't have to try at all. It was the last time that I would see Trog but not the last time that I would hear his name when my punk past would come back to haunt me at the Heritage Hotel.

The arrest for assault and robbery happened one night when I was returning to Stanmore by taxi from the city with a Kiwi punk named Jim. We were used to catching taxis back from the city and stopping on the opposite side of Stanmore station so we could do a runner through the pedestrian tunnel. On this particular night Kiwi Jim decided not to run when the cab driver chased us but instead waited in the tunnel to take him on. I went back to stop him doing anything stupid and luckily the driver decided that the small fare was not worth risking his life for and left. Jim was pissed off and wanted to go after him but I talked him out of it and we went for a walk instead. We walked up to Parramatta Road and wandered around looking for a drink. The only place opened was an all-night florist. We walked past the florist and up to the next corner where Jim told me to wait. He went back down the road and I was too tired to care what he was doing. After several minutes I went to look for him and almost ran into a guy running out of the florist. The guy ran out onto Parramatta road waving his hands in the air trying to stop the traffic. After a few seconds Jim came running out of the same shop and we took off up the road together. I assumed that he had tried to break into the till and steal some money We ran around a corner and down a side street before pausing to catch our breath. We stood for a while trying to figure out the quickest way back to the house at Stanmore. We weren't standing there long when three unmarked police cars came screaming down the road. They screeched to a halt beside us and several detectives jumped out with guns at the ready and threw us to the ground.

We were taken in separate cars back to Annandale police station. They told me that they were members of the Armed Hold Up Squad. The Armed Hold Up Squad were known as the Breakers and they were Roger Rogerson's boys. Rogerson has recently been convicted of murder but everyone on the streets in the seventies and early eighties knew that he was a stone-cold killer. I don't know whether he was one of the arresting officers but all the way to the station all they talked about was whether to kill me or lock me up. They only decided to let me live when I told them that I had family. I've met a lot of hard men in my time but these guys were the most cold-blooded killers I have ever met. The casual way that they discussed tossing my body off the Sydney harbor heads made my blood run cold. They had been up the road on a stakeout but the villains had failed to show up. They were very pleased that their night had not been completely wasted and were more than happy to take out their frustration on us. They were like cats playing with a mouse and they couldn't wait to go in for the kill.

Once we had arrived at the police station I was handcuffed in the dock. They then tried the nice guy bad guy routine on me. I thought that this was really funny because I had seen it on the television so many times. I played along for a while before telling them that I knew exactly what they were doing and that they must be really dumb to think that anyone would fall for such a stupid routine. The situation got even funnier as they suffered role reversal and the nice guy had to be calmed down by the bad guy. They then took me into an interview room and handcuffed me to a chair in the middle of the room. They took turns slapping me about the body with phone books. I eventually pretended to crack and cry so they would leave me alone. My mistake was laughing as soon as they had left the room. I looked up and noticed that the top of the wall was surrounded by tiny mirrors and knew that I was in trouble. The door burst open and the cops burst in even angrier than had been before. They threw the chair down and dragged me around on the ground before sitting me up and slapping me with phone books again.

Later they brought in a confession supposedly signed by Jim. It sounded like it had been written by some sixty's stoner. They had used words like 'man' and 'cool' and 'baby' and I couldn't help but laugh. They kept coming back with revised editions of the same story being told by different characters. I kept telling them how wrong they were until I realised that I may have been inadvertently helping them and decided to shut up. I had been locked up many times before for drunk and disorderly and released in the morning without charge. The cops were operating under a quota system in those days and they were more interested in numbers than in seriously solving crimes. I didn't realise that I was in real trouble until they brought in the guy from the florists. He a bandage around his arm and they told me that he had been stabbed. The cops told me that they were charging with being an accessory to assault and robbery and I didn't think that it was funny anymore. I was still only seventeen so they had to call my parents. The worst thing was the look on their faces when they came to take me home. They showed up looking like ghosts and I spent the next nine months on bail dreading the prospect of doing hard time. The cops verballed me when we finally did get to trial claiming that I had confessed on the way to the police station. Sometimes the people that everyone thinks are the good guys are actually the bad guys, life can be funny like that!

CHAPTER 5

The punk ritual evolved along with the bands and the population. The ritual involved the annihilation of ego in a pogoing frenzy that was the forerunner of the modern day mosh pit. Punters would leap high into the air and collide in midflight. It was both a friendly handshake and a bloodless battle. It was designed to disrupt and disturb but not necessarily to injure. It was also a friendly reminder that nothing was set and anarchy could arrive at any moment. You were never alone and never safe and you must give up your sense of self and certainty to the mass movement or risk being bounced into oblivion. There was no stage diving because there was no stage and there were no footlights or foldback to divide the punters from the performers. This is an essential difference between ritual and spectacle outlined by performance theorists like Richard Schechner.

The punk ritual operated upon the same lines as all successful rituals. Just as a séance needs the total compliance and confidence of those involved in order to summon spirits so the punk performance demanded total commitment in order for it to work. The difference between the punk ritual and most other successful rituals is that while most rituals are performed to instill belief the punk ritual was performed to annihilate all such sentiments. The punk ritual was not performed for the greater glory of the band. The band was just a part of the performance. It was not a celebration of celebrity but a celebration of the cessation of such servitude. The ritual was so intense that it generated an energy that was palpable. It scared heretics away and kept sceptics at bay. The lack of any discernable doctrine made the movement difficult to understand. Any half-hearted excursion into its mysteries was doomed to disaster. The punk scene could not be experienced by testing the waters with your toe but demanded full immersion. The negation of self that the performance entailed was like death. Once embraced it granted the participant the freedom to truly live without fear. It was everything and it was nothing. It was Nirvana!

After the ritual had been performed and everyone was free from everything we would gather on the footpath and plot our next public punk performance. The mass movement of punks through the streets at this time was exhilarating and soon led to many adventures. The earliest of these was to trendy parties run by rich people living in inner city suburbs. For the rich people whose homes we invaded it must have been like some crazy clown act had come to perform at their party. For us it meant free food and drink and the chance to scare the pants off people. A girl named Jessica dominated these early outings. She was tall and thin with short dark hair and loads of poise and charismatic cool. I was so impressed with her that I later named my eldest daughter after her. She was elegant and intelligent but also rich so she always knew where the best parties were being held. We would pile out of the Native Rose and pile into Paul with a car's car. With arms and legs hanging out of windows we would fly through the streets hurling abuse and bottles at passersby. Drunk driving wasn't illegal back then and unless you actually ran into something you were generally pretty safe from the law. Those who could not cram into the cars would throw in whatever cash they had and hail taxis. It was always possible to convince some poor driver into breaking the law and taking as many punks as possible as long as you had the cash.

One early party that we attended was at a hall in Darlinghurst that was full of drag queens. There were crazy costumes and big wigs everywhere and we were feeling a little lost and underdressed. We were used to being the outrageous ones but could not compete with this extreme level of camp. It seemed as if we would simply have to slink away until someone put New Rose by The Damned on the record player. Punks piled onto the dance floor and started to perform our now familiar ritual. The drag queens tried valiantly to hold the dance floor but all attempts to quell the power of the pogo proved impossible. When one of the terrible twins set fire to the streamers covering the ceiling all hell broke loose. The threat that the flames presented to the fabulous fabric and fake hair sent all of the drag queens screaming from the dance floor. We were fighting for our space on the cultural dance floor and were finally winning the room.

The most memorable of these early excursions was to a block of flats in Rose Bay. The flats were almost empty and were being slowly renovated floor by floor. Scaffolding covered the walls like a steel skeleton. The inside was barren except for dust and dirt and the occasional bag of hard cement. We ascended the stairs in silence until we arrived at the top flat which the owners had already occupied. There wasn't much room in the apartment and all of the available floor space was covered with bean bags and Avant guard trash. At first our presence was greeted with the usual interest and excitement. This was soon turned to reticence and resentment as we overwhelmed the small space and quickly debilitated the limited supply of food and alcohol. Panic soon set in and the owners began threatening to call the police. We removed the phone and ourselves and what remained of the food and alcohol to the floor below. Our former hosts must have felt quite triumphant for a short time. They decided to barricade themselves in the flat before realising that they had now become prisoners at their own party.

Our own party continued on the floor below with much drinking and singing and dancing until we heard our hosts screaming for help from the windows above. Several punks lent out the widows and threw bottles up at them. Others began dismantling the scaffolding to try and force them back inside with the long steel poles. These poles then inevitably began falling into the street and caused considerable damage to the cars parked below. Scaffolding was soon being hurled into the streets and windows were being smashed and eventually sirens were heard wailing in the background. The entire balustrade on the stairs was systematically dismantled as we descended to the street smashing and singing as we went. We escaped in the usual way of jumping fences and running through back yards. It was a miracle that no one ever got arrested or seriously injured during these escapades. We behaved like destructive demons and had anarchic angles on our shoulders.

This party started a cultural phenomenon known as the 'Destroy Party'. Destroy parties were held whenever someone was evicted or their lease expired or sometimes just for the fun of it. The house at Stanmore was later left with holes in the walls and garbage piled so high that you had to walk over it rather than wade through it. A house we lived in later in Newtown was almost totally demolished while we were still living in it. The first Destroy Party will always be the best as it was totally unexpected and the sheer size of the structure gave the legend legs. There would be many destroy parties in the future but the future hadn't happened yet.

What did happen was the opening of a new disco in George Street almost opposite the movie theatres. This monstrosity was called Max's and demonstrated all the Hollywood glitz and glamour that Punk opposed. It was like a succubus successfully suckering kids from the suburbs into a world of mindless consumerism. Standing sweating on the footpath outside the Grand Hotel we decided that we were obliged to confront this new and horrifying evil.

We moved with one mind toward the abomination without any real understanding what we would do. Half way up George Street divine inspiration struck in the form of an adult entertainment store. It is impossible to remember details in such transcendent moments but I suspect it was Rod the Rodent or Chris Cross who first entered the store and started trying on the perverted apparel. Soon all the punks were cramming through the doors and fighting over blow up dolls and dildos. The guy behind the counter was powerless to prevent our pilfering and was probably wise not to try. We purloined as much pornographic paraphernalia as we could carry and left the store proudly displaying our trophies to continue our militant march up the hill.

We stood on the footpath opposite the disco defiantly waving our sex toys in the air while screaming our war cries like an army about to go into battle. Pedestrians paused and traffic stopped as we cavorted on the side of the road. As soon as we had attracted as much attention as possible someone yelled 'charge!' We hurtled across the road and ran up the stairs outside the disco. Suburban kids dressed in their best Saturday night tights screamed and ran for cover. The bouncers tried to restrain us but we were like a plague of locusts that could not be contained or controlled. An enemy that they would not have imagined in their worst nightmares was overwhelming their surroundings and their sense of certainty. They were being assaulted by blow up dolls and dildos as much as by punks and had no idea how to respond. Feather bowers were tripping their legs and tangling their hands as they tried in vain to assert some order. They were lashed with leather whips and lathered in various lubricating lotions and were eventually overwhelmed by the sheer ridiculousness of the situation. This was the theatre of violence. We were not there to beat their bodies but to molest their minds. I remember running into the foyer which was separated from the disco by glass doors. The disco dummies had run to the doors to see what was happening. The look of terror upon their faces was truly pathetic and absolutely priceless. Thoughtless consumers assaulted by anarchy. They may have ended up spending a thousand nights amidst the humdrum decadence of disco but this is the one night that they would remember. The cops were soon there as the Central police station was just around the corner. As usual they were too late to prevent the performance and too slow to catch the culprits.

The other pastime that became prevalent at this time, whatever time this was, was the trip to the airport to say goodbye to people going on their pilgrimage to the holy sites in London. Johnny Dole had left searching for streets paved with gold and some of the Scabs soon followed. Short Bob had left far too early and was rumoured to be living in an all black room with nothing but a pentagram for company. He later formed a band called Blood and Roses and got his face on the cover of Melody Maker. Bob told me later that once he became famous, he realized that he didn't really want to be. If he really wanted to play punk and not be famous, he really should have stayed in Australia. Others soon followed him overseas, including Andy and Ross Guerilla, but not before they performed more farewell gigs than anyone in the history of rock n' roll with Danny Rumour on guitar. Trips to the airport became such a regular occurrence that the Federal Police were on a first name basis with some of us. They eventually realised that if we were left alone, we would eventually leave. If they hassled us then we would hassle them and forty or fifty punks were more trouble than we were worth.

The time I remember most fondly was when Cathi got arrested. We were all gathered in the upstairs bar happily drinking jugs of cheap beer when two federal police officers came in and ordered drinks. They leant against the bar nonchalantly. They were trying hard to be inconspicuous but had very large two-way radios attached to the back of their belts. The thing that annoyed us most was not this obvious insult to our intelligence but that they were really rude. Each time a punk would go to the bar they would say 'afternoon officer' and offer to buy them a beer. The police refused our hospitality and even ignored our attempts to make friends. They were so rude that we decided to leave without even bothering to finish our drinks. Chris Cross had come up with a plan and we stood as one and headed for the escalator. The police waited several seconds before following. This delay placed them on top of the down escalator just as we were reaching the bottom. We were then able to get on the up escalator and wave to them as they passed by. The police were not deterred from their duty and ran to the bottom of the escalator in order to follow us up. We then jumped on the down escalator in order to wave at them again as they went up. This continued for longer than anyone could believe and was so funny that punks kept falling off the escalators laughing. Our beer was flat by the time we got back to the bar.

The detectives eventually decided to join us in the bar us and bought us beers. This attempt at détente made Cathi mad. Cathi really hated cops because her real last name was so common that they always thought that she was giving an alias when she was questioned. She got so sick of the harassment that she once gave an alias at the Grand Hotel and was subsequently arrested for a warrant on the fake name. She could not abide the police buying us beers and left the bar screaming abuse at everybody. The cops asked us to stay put while they did their job which was something that they did really badly.

Cathi went down the stairs yelling at the top of her lungs with the Feds squawking almost as loudly into their two-way radios as they followed. We followed behind at a safe distance taking our beers with us because the cops were too distracted by the animated corpse to notice what we were doing.

Cathi got to the ground floor and seeing that she was surrounded by cops she took off her gun belt. The gun belt was filled with live 303 rounds and was Cathi's weapon of choice. She started swinging the belt around her head to keep the cops at bay. She then took out a bullet and threatened to throw it like it was a hand grenade. The cops were uncertain and circled her for some time. There were no Tasers in those days so their options were limited. The absurd sight soon attracted a considerable crowd and the crowd was cheering for Cathi. Sheer embarrassment eventually forced the cops into action. They rushed Cathi and managed to wrestle her to the ground. She was taken to a cell somewhere that she swears was padded. The cops came out when the crowd had disbursed and asked us to leave. We told them that we really couldn't go until we knew what was happening to Cathi. We knew that they couldn't arrest all of us because they simply did not have the numbers or the facilities. We decided to stage a 'sit in' in the middle of the airport. This standoff was something that they did not expect. It was so far outside their limited field of expertise that decided to give in almost instantly. Cathi came out with arms raised in victory and we all went back to the bar to celebrate.

Another once upon a time we were in the upstairs bar when Cathi Corpse and Rod Rodent came rolling in on wheelchairs. They were both so thin and pale that no one would have questioned whether they were really incapacitated. When someone playfully questioned Rod about his illness he replied with one word, 'Gallipoli. It was Anzac Day and there did not seem to be a more fitting memorial to the disastrous World War One campaign than a corpse and a rat in wheelchairs. We drank several schooners to the departed diggers with the utmost respect before someone decided that they should race the wheelchairs down the escalators. Cathi wasn't too keen but as several other punks offered to take her place, she decided to go through with the challenge rather than give up her seat. As we approached the top of the escalators the federal police intervened. When they questioned Rod and Cathi about their use of the wheelchairs Rod replied with the single secular word that is most holy in the Australian lexicon, Gallipoli.

The police were taken aback but one did manage to point out that they were both far too young to have been at Gallipoli. Chris Cross was pushing Rod's chair at the time and replied almost instantly, 'But Gallipoli is for everybody.' Everyone then joined in the protest by repeating the phrase as a chorus with just a hint of self-righteous indignation. As the police pondered their position Cathi made a break for it and rolled away as fast as she could. The cops turned to chase her just as Chris Cross decided to push Rod's wheelchair down the escalator. Everyone stood in fearful fascination as the chair bumped and bounced its way to the bottom. The chair and its occupant threatened to topple over on several occasions but it was kept relatively stable by the side railings and Rod's desperate attempts to hold on. When he finally did hit the ground, he skidded out of the wheelchair and along the slippery tiles as the chair crashed across the hard-concrete floor. We held our collective breathe for several seconds until Rod jumped to his feet and raised his arms in the air declaring, 'It's a miracle, I can walk, It's a Gallipoli miracle!' We all ran down to celebrate the miracle and left the cops confounded at the top of the stairs. We then went back to the bar to continue our celebrations.

CHAPTER 6

Rejex eventually got good enough to play at the centre of the ritual at the Grand Hotel. Our first few performances were too bad for even punks to appreciate. The most popular song that we performed was called Eskyland. It had a slow bouncy rhythm that was perfect for the pogo followed by a thrashy chorus so everyone could go nuts. The best exponent of the pogo was a punk named Fenton. Fenton was a big freckled-faced monster from England. He had a Union Jack permanently and proudly displayed on the back of his shirt. He was sweet and gentle by nature but could use his broad shoulders to destroy anyone on the dance floor. I remember Fenton entering the poolroom of the Grand Hotel one night just in time to witness someone hitting Greg Dog over the head with a pool cue. Fenton turned them around and hit them under the chin so hard that they flew through the air and landed on their back on top of the pool table. Fenton was fine until he realised that he had hit a feminist who only looked like a man. We all thought it was pretty funny but Fenton was so upset that we didn't see him for weeks.

The Last Words didn't last long and The Broken Toys broke up. We were looking for bands and as I was wandering down George Street one night when I found one. There were two lost souls in black leather and studs with bleached blonde hair looking for a home. Their names were Mark and Con and they were from

Wollongong. I told them about the Grand Hotel but they said they'd been there but it wasn't what they were looking for. They told me that they played Sex Pistols covers and I told them they'd be laughed off stage in Sydney. I told them to write some originals and I'd get them a gig. The first time that they played at the Grand as Suicide Squad the band room was empty. Everyone was still in the bar or the poolroom chatting. I felt bad for the band and raced into the poolroom to announce that the Flintstones had escaped from the cartoon world and were now playing punk. It wasn't that far from the truth as Mark did look like Barney Rubble. He had short blonde spiked hair to match his short stocky body. He was a natural guitar player and proved to be the perfect punk performer. Con was a gentle giant who looked more like Bam than Bam Bam and played the bass. The singer was overweight with short curly black hair slicked back with grease and only needed a leopard skin leotard to complete his undeniable resemblance to Fred Flintstone. The drummer earned the name Dino by default. He had longish red hair and was as friendly as his cartoon namesake. Punks crowded into the band room and soon realized that the resemblance was real. The similarity with the cartoon characters did not last long. A big brassy, blonde dominatrix named Annie soon replaced Fred. Annie had a presence that was bigger than the band. She worked for a hard-core porno mag called Ribald which matched her sense of humour and personality perfectly. With Annie up front Suicide Squad soon became really great punk rock performers.

Another band that became an integral part of the scene were The Section who grew up about two miles from where I had lived in the Western Suburbs but who I didn't meet until they came to the Grand Hotel. The Section were formed around another set of brothers, Mick and Vern, who were the sons of English immigrants and still carried slight accents. They were good-looking boys with square jaws, rocker haircuts and competing sideburns. Mick sang and Vern played guitar while a straight looking guy named Mills played the bass. Charley played the drums and had as much raw talent as he had tattoos. He was a wiry Maltese warrior from Greystanes and later played with me in Rejex and Vellocette. After I met the band at the Grand, they asked if I would come out and hear them rehearse to see if they could get a gig. They picked me up from Outside the Housing Commission in Parramatta where I was working and we drove to a house in Greystanes. They had a bedroom set up as a band room. They played some Sex Pistols songs and a few other covers. Their musicianship was excellent but I told them the same thing that I had told Suicide Squad. They had to write originals if they wanted to be taken seriously in the Sydney scene. They agreed to do this and we all drove back into town to celebrate. Parramatta road was the road that most people took to the punk scene. It runs from the working-class west to Broadway and the heart of the city. Another group who followed this path to punk paradise were Chaos.

Chaos were Blacktown boys born and bred. Colin Chaos was very tall and very thin and had curly red hair with matching freckles covering extremely pale skin. He believed that people with red hair were descended from Vikings and played his Gibson SG like a warrior's axe. Borgy was a solidly built bloke who played the bass. He had short-cropped black hair and big brown eyes and while Collin's face was thin and all angles Borgy's was as round as a new born babe. He played his bass slung so low that he could hardly reach it and his furious fretwork perfectly matched Colin's chaotic guitar riffs. Dave was a short and solid with wavy brown hair and was very mild mannered unless he was playing the drums. The captain of the crew was Kevin Chaos or Captain Chaotic as he preferred to be called. Captain Kev had the crooked posture and gnarly features of old man but had the attitude and enthusiasm of a small child. He had stringy blonde hair and the jaded look of a junky and was famous for uttering such silly sentiments as 'you can't be a punk rocker if you don't love Led Zeppelin'.

Chaos came with their own chaotic culture and several serious supporters. These included Trish and Bib who quite rightly got quite upset when I called them groupies. There was also Little Rob, Rob Millionaire and his friend Ross Meathead. There wasn't much of Little Rob but it was all cheeky. He was like a bow-legged bantam with a flat top hairdo and side burns. He had been living in London which gave him instant credibility. He brought with him a Gibson guitar and a Marshal amp but preferred to play with tarot cards. Little Rob was Mr. Magic and went on to join several esoteric organisations after Punk. Many punks believed that he used his occult powers to seduce women because he was so successful. He was no male model but Rob was full of wit and one liners and didn't need magic to get lucky.

My favourite Little Rob story was when we were at a party in Pyrmont when a guy named Colin Pill got dressed up in a gorilla suit. The party was pretty slow so we decided it would be fun to go gorilla hunting. We went around the party gathering cigarette lighters and adjusting the flames to full throttle. When we had enough firepower, we told Colin what we intended because it wouldn't have been fun unless we got him to run. He was hesitant at first but when we demonstrated our willingness to burn him right there and then he took off out of the door. One kind soul was so concerned for his safety that they filled up a bucket of water so they could put him out when we finally did catch up with him. We chased him out of the house and down the street screaming and flicking the flames of our lighters. Colin ran ahead at full pace until he came to a corner and froze. We caught up to him and saw what had stopped him in his tracks. Little Rob was banging a girl up against a wall in full view of the traffic on the nearby overpass. The kind soul with the bucket of water then ran up and threw the contents all over them. Rob turned around and with his trade mark cheeky grin said, 'I feel like a randy dog.' We decided to set fire to Colin Pill to celebrate!

There was also Rob Millionaire who earned his nickname because he had a job and a car. He was also called Bob the Boner because he worked at an abattoir. He had a head that seemed like the skin was stretched straight over the skull with no meat in between. He was all sinews and tattoos and had the hollow eyes and haunted look of a junky long before anyone was using. Rob's ghoul like exterior belied a calm disposition that was rarely ruffled. He was always willing to listen to what anyone had to say about anything. He had been a drug dealer in Blacktown and became the go to man for pot and acid in the punk scene for the next few years. Rob's best mate was Ross Meathead who was a skinny kid of Scottish descent who had curly steel wool for hair. He got this nasty nickname from Fat Chris and wasn't meat head enough to argue. Fat Chris had recently played prop forward for the Blacktown football team so he was fat like a tank. He had curly brown hair, the face of a chubby cherub and hands like sledgehammers. Chris was one of those big guys who didn't know whether to be tough or funny so he could make you laugh your head off while he was beating your brains in.

The other important figure was Crasti who was an artistic prodigy. He had won the Australian Art Award for his H.S.C painting. He proved that he was as crazy as he was gifted by giving up his art in order to become a full time punk. Crasti was lean and mean and had a terrible temper. The worst night that I spent as a punk came when he decided to take his temper out for a drink one night at the Oxford Hotel. He came with Colin Chaos and they were sculling rum while I was sipping beer. We started playing pool against a group of Italian boys who lived locally and dealt drugs at the Tradesman's Arms Hotel in Woolloomooloo. They were taking the night off by taking their girlfriends out for a good time. While the drug dealers were there to make love Crasti was there to make trouble. He ranted and raved and did everything he could to start a fight other than just hitting one of them over the head with a pool cue. He was so drunk that they thought of him more as a figure of fun than a threat which made him even madder. I was still sober and only stayed to keep the peace. Colin was too drunk to help and Crasti was too drunk to help himself.

I was really relieved when the pub finally closed. We walked out into the cold night air and waited for the traffic lights to change. The cold night air also woke Crasti up and gave him a second wind. Just as the lights changed and I thought that we were out of trouble he started again. The Italians were doing their best to ignore him while I did my best to try and drag him away. Crasti was like a dog with a bone and would not let it go. He got so upset that his nose started to bleed and he managed to splatter blood all over one of the girlfriend's dresses. You could feel the change in the air like you can when a storm is coming. The tentative laughter had turned into a terrible tension and I grabbed Colin and Crasti and took off around the corner. I was thinking that only half of them were likely to follow and if we could put some space between us and them, we might have had half a chance. We were outnumbered by four to one and only one of us was sober enough to fight but I had only gone about ten yards when I realised that I was on my own.

I knew that going back was suicide but also that continuing to run was unthinkable. I turned back to find that only one of the Italian guys had followed me. We stood staring at each other for a second before he picked up one of the lead weights that held down the newspapers on the corner. I realised that he couldn't grab me with that hand so I ran at his right shoulder. To my surprise he didn't try to stop me but turned and ran back around the corner. I followed hard on his heels in a reversal of roles that would have been comical if the situation wasn't so serious. When we got around the corner, I saw Colin being crucified up against a telegraph pole with two of the hoods holding his arms while another punched him in the ribs. Crasti was surrounded out on the street but was still on his feet. The guy I was chasing then ran straight at Colin and hit him square in the face with the lead weight. Colin's mouth exploded with teeth and blood flying everywhere. The violence of the impact was so shocking that everybody froze and I took the opportunity to grab Colin and start dragging him across Oxford Street. I was yelling at Crasti to follow but his temper had him trapped. I don't know if it was a death wish or some kind of death before dishonour Blacktown code. It seemed insane at the time and still does today. I stood on the opposite corner for a while wondering whether I should drop Colin and go back for Crasti. I decided that if he didn't want to leave, I couldn't make him so I couldn't see the point. I ended up carrying Colin down to a shared house in Bourke Street where Les was living. I waited while he did what he could to stop the bleeding before calling an ambulance. For years Colin and Crasti told people that I had simply run away because they couldn't remember what actually happened. I still don't know if I did right or wrong and the night still haunts me. It does prove that you be both a hero and a coward in the same circumstances, life can be really unfunny like that!

CHAPTER 7

Punk in Sydney was a philosophical musical movement. It was the creation of a vacuum to reflect what we saw as the centre of modern western consumer culture. We parodied the meaningless of society by becoming its most meaningless component. This is why no one on the outside was able to understand what was happening. Being inexplicable was the whole point of Punk. The only fundamental rule was fun. The Sydney punk scene was a very exclusive club because you had to be smart enough to get the joke. If you did not get the joke you were the joke! This was why people found the culture so difficult to define because the very essence of the philosophy was to defy such certainty. People are truly scared of the unknown. We were determined to be totally unknowable even to ourselves. Hapless punters who wandered in to the Grand Hotel hoping to join the movement were assaulted by spit and wit until all sense of certainty or self was overwhelmed by meaningless juvenile joy. When Little Chris Faye turned up, he was totally immersed in spit on four occasions and pissed on once before his perseverance was finally rewarded with begrudging acceptance.

In the early days there was never more than fifty punks at any one time but this number had grown to around a hundred by 1978. The order in which people appeared or disappeared is not as important as the fact that they were there and a part of the story that was

Punk. I cannot remember everyone because my memory is too mediocre or they were too mediocre to be remembered. There were people like Hegarty who was a short guy with a permanent five o'clock shadow. He had the calm disposition of an account but had decided to defy his D.N.A and become a punk. Hegarty demonstrated that it was not always how crazy you looked on the outside that counted. There are a few more personalities that must be mentioned. Like Hardware, House brick and Karl who were all rejects from the Navy. Hardware had the worst acne that I have ever seen. He is remembered fondly by me for one incident in particular when he spent a good ten minutes rolling a joint. This was because a group of girls, including the luscious Sexy Sue, were hassling him to hurry. Sexy Sue was almost as big as her breasts. She was a bombshell blonde with cat eye makeup. She became the archetype for many of the young punk girls in the scene. Sometimes it seemed like you were surrounded by pretty blonde midgets all giggling through dark red lipstick. These included Wendy, Shirley and Kay Quail. Kay was cute and looks as good now as she did in the day. She recently organised a punk reunion for Cathi Corpse and was universally acclaimed as the most wonderful girl in the world. When Hardware eventually finished rolling the joint, he sucked it slowly through his acne-scarred lips, sliming it up so that it would burn slow. The impatience of the girls reached fever pitch as he sucked the joint into his mouth one last time before swallowing it whole. He then licked his lips with relish as the frustrated girls screamed their disappointment and almost ripped him to shreds.

The other group of importance were from Brisbane and were led by V2. They brought with them politics and an addiction to downers. V2 was famous for falling off his chair while declaring that 'the kids are having fun!'. Brisbane Punk politics revolved around the laws in Queensland at the time prohibiting the right to march. They boasted endlessly about how they had taken part in marches against the anti-marching law. This would have been fine if they thought it was funny but was sad because they took it so seriously. The idea of punks taking part in any organised response to anything or even being organised at all was against everything that we didn't believe in. It took some time to persuade them of the error of their ways and get them to accept the righteousness of disbelief but they did inspire the lyrics to Rejex impending single "Who wants to march when you can riot." Which was an attempt to sum up the sentiments of the Sydney scene at the time.

There may have been over a hundred punks in the Sydney scene but there were still a lot more police than there were punks. Sometimes on a slow night at the Grand Hotel we would have more police than punks in the place. In the early days we would have bail parties when someone was arrested. Everyone would put in whatever change they had and a volunteer would go to the desk sergeant and offer it as a bribe. The quota system meant that anyone could be arrested at any time without any real reason. Punks often spent the evening with a bunch of homeless people, crazies and winos who were all there just to make up the numbers. We didn't bail people out because they were in serious trouble but because it could get really unpleasant amidst all the vomit and madness. One such occasion involved a massive police raid by plain clothed detectives who were waiting outside the Grand Hotel at closing time. They didn't look like cops and had failed to disclose their status. They grabbed Animal and he managed to knock a few of them to the ground before they restrained him. It was only when they put the on cuffs that he realized that they were cops. We held a bail party and I volunteered to take the bribe to the police station. The desk sergeant was not happy to see me because the whole operation was a bit of a debacle. I asked him if Animal was in the cells and he told me that he was but he was staying there because the charge was serious. I asked him what the charge was and he told me that he couldn't tell me. He could tell me that I would be joining him in the cells if I didn't shut up and get out. I thought he was just in a bad mood and I tried to cheer him up by offering the bribe but this only seemed to make him madder. I realised that the situation was serious because I had never heard of a police officer refusing a bribe before. I decided to push my luck by making some stupid joke about a possible early release for good behavior. This made him so angry that he managed to heave his rather large frame up out of his chair and make a sad attempt at leaping the front counter. I was out the door before he left his chair and if it hadn't been for some young gun chasing me half way down Harris Street, I would have got away clean.

I got locked up in a cell just across from Animal and woke him up by calling out his name as quietly as I could. He told me that the cops were upset because he had broken one on their wristwatches in the struggle. He thought he would probably have to make an appearance before a magistrate. An opinion that was soon verified by the cop in question when he came down the corridor to tell us to shut up. He then whined for several seconds about the wristwatch in question being a birthday present from his mother. Animal could not believe that the cop was being such a sook and told him so in no uncertain terms. The cop told Animal that he was going to be charged with public affray and assaulting a police officer as well as damaging his wrist watch. He then said that if I didn't shut up then I would be joining him in the dock. This effectively ended our conversation and I went to sleep on the bare boards that impersonated a bed in the lockups in those days.

I was woken up later by the sound of someone singing. I looked out of my cell to see Bailey walking down the corridor swinging a large set of keys on a chain. He was banging them against the cell doors as if he owned the place. It took me several seconds of vigorous eye rubbing before I was convinced that I was not dreaming. I called out and he let out of my cell explaining that there had been a shift change. He said that the new cops were more sympathetic but he still couldn't get Animal out. We woke Animal up anyway so I could give him the bail money and wish him good luck. Bailey then escorted me up to the front room where the cops were drinking a bottle of confiscated scotch while playing cards. The sergeant was apparently banging a girlfriend of Bailey's in a closet down the hall. We sat down to have a drink and wait for Bailey's friend to finish up. The coppers were cracking jokes with Bailey like they were the best of friends. The phone finally rang and the police were told that an inspector was on the way. Bailey's friend came out of the broom closet straightening her clothes and the three of us left with the bottle of confiscated scotch. I don't know how Bailey managed to weave such magic. He had the gift of the gab but something special besides that was probably obtained in some clandestine deal with the devil at the crossroads at midnight. We walked back home drinking the scotch and singing songs while celebrating the general weirdness of the world.

I ended up spending the night in every police station in inner city Sydney over the next few years. This included being locked up one night for drunk and disorderly when I was stone cold sober. I was walking through the Cross with a couple of private school girls and their male companion. A bull wagon pulled up and the coppers started dragging a prostrate wino into the back of the van. The guy we were with decided to tell the coppers off before I could slap some sense into him. I was hoping the cops might overlook it and kept walking as casually as I could. They must have been short of numbers because they stopped us just up the road. I told them I was sober and that they should arrest one of the girls as they were drunk. It did me no good and I was hauled off to Darlinghurst Police Station. I was locked in a cell with the idiot who started the whole thing. he complained the whole time that his dad was a lawyer and that they were the ones who were in trouble. I eventually had to threaten to kill him in order to shut him up and went to sleep on the boards without further trouble. When I woke up in the morning the guy was gone. I yelled out to the sergeant to let me out. I asked him what had happened to the young guy and he told me that his father had been a lawyer and had come to get him out. When I asked why he didn't get me out he said that the kid had told them that he didn't know me very well. This was another reason why rich kids shouldn't be punks, they had no manners at all. They say that revenge is a dish best served cold and this particular dish sat on the counter for some time before I was able to taste it so you will also have to wait as well.

The time that Pommy Ian and I were held at the Circular Quay lockup was my favourite. We were at some gig down near the water seeing some band that featured a clown up front but they weren't very funny. We were walking home when someone removed a circular lampshade from a streetlight and started up a soccer game in the street. It was all harmless fun but got quite competitive so we were too involved to get out of the way when a car came. The occupant of the car had to wait several seconds before there was a pause in play. This would not have tested the patience of most people but the driver of this particular vehicle turned out to be a police inspector. Several minutes later a paddy wagon pulled up and the police officers wanted to confiscate our ball. Ian and I were fighting over possession of the ball at the time and refused to give it up. We were subsequently arrested and taken to the cop station at Circular Quay. We were then displayed as trophies before the inspector who had obviously stayed around to gloat. He seemed more upset than was really warranted and had just decided to send us to the cells for the evening when all the other punks came down the road singing an English soccer song that went:

Standing on a corner swinging my chain,
Up came a copper and he asked my name,
I kicked him in the balls and kicked him in the head,
Now that copper is dead, La la la etc.

The cops were so incensed by this act of pretended hooliganism that they tried to arrest everybody and took us all into a large room at the back of the station. They lined us all up in front of a desk and started trying to take down our names. The first person to front the desk gave his name as Vic Vomit but the cop was too sharp for this and told him that this was not his real name. Vic's mate Paul was next in line and verified the cop's suspicions by admitting that he was the real Vic Vomit. Another punk then began arguing with Paul claiming that he was also an imposter and they were the real Vic Vomit. Pandemonium soon broke loose as all of the punks in the room argued animatedly about who was the real Vic vomit. Threats were made and slaps exchanged as the cops tried valiantly but in vain to restore some sense of order to their station. The fact that we did not believe the sign on the wall that said 'police read' upset them even more. As they steadfastly refused to disprove our suspicion by reading the posted information, we felt justified in our assertion that they could not really read. The police soon realised that they had taken on more than they could chew and told us to leave. We instead insisted on being charged and told them that they would be neglecting their duty if they let us go. We demanded to talk to whoever was in charge and started singing again to emphasise our right to be arrested. The inspector who had started the whole trouble then came in and actually apologised to us and even gave back our ball. He shook our hands like a good referee should at the conclusion of a good game. We all left feeling vindicated and continued our game and our singing all the way home.

The strangest encounter with the cops was one night when we were going to Roger Thought Criminals' place in Woolloomooloo.

There were about a dozen of us and we were all tripping heavily. We walked through Hyde Park while calling each other Kowalski and pretending to fire machine guns like we were in an American war movie. When we got down to the harbour and turned the corner outside the hotel we saw a police wagon parked by the side of the road. Two police officers were standing on the footpath facing us. They had taken off their hats, badges and gun belts and had locked them in the van. No one knew what to do so we just kept walking. No one spoke and the only sound was our steel cap boots crunching on the concrete. We could smell something fishy and knew that it wasn't coming from the harbor. There was no way that two unarmed police officers were going to win such a contest unless they had reserves around the corner. We all knew that it was a trap without saying a word. The coppers tensed as we passed silently by them totally ignoring their presence. We walked around the corner before stopping and staring at each other in silent disbelief. The whole scenario was so unreal that it was hard to believe that it happened. The effects of the acid were so severe that no one seemed certain whether we were just suffering from a mass hallucination.

The hostility that the police held for punk was way out of proportion to the problems that punks caused. It was like they actually believed that we were an active anarchist organization. Les Wreckage and I were walking down the street one night when we were arrested for doing nothing at all. They took us to Darlinghurst police station and made Les take off every single safety pin as if they were weapons. Les had a lot of safety pins and he counted each one as he handed them over. There was no police station in the Cross in those days so Darlinghurst handled everything. A young guy was beaten to death in Darlinghurst one night and the police said that he had Fallen down the stairs. I don't remember there being any stairs between the front desk and the cells. There were stairs leading down to tunnels underneath but no one was ever locked up there overnight. When Les and I were released in the morning Les took his time and made sure that every single safety pin was returned and replaced before he would leave. The police were not pleased but Les was pissed off and persistent. We walked out together but considering the corruption and contempt of the cops it was a miracle that we were walking out at all.

CHAPTER 8

I had moved out of home after finishing High School and attended Sydney University for a brief time studiously avoiding studying political science. I got a job because my lawyer told me the courts viewed students as dole bludgers with books. If Punk was a theatre of violence then the law was the theatre of justice. The court was a performance space. The lawyers were actors doing their best to impress the judge and jury. That the future of the accused was in the balance seemed a secondary concern at best. My parents had taken out a lone to pay for my barrister. He was a big burly man who was all bluff and bluster. His bombastic tone and bold manner was well suited to the role of the leading man. He courted the court with urbane humour as he derided his opposition with a weary patience and a condescending tone. The prosecutor was a small angry man with dark curly hair who was rumoured to have political aspirations. He could not control his temper or his contempt for the courtly theatrics of his adversary. He had therefore inadvertently cast himself as the bad guy and was never going to win.

The tactics employed in my defence seemed to consist of a bellicose laugh timed to interrupt anything that the prosecutor said and in response to anything that the police offered in evidence. It also seemed that the judge allowed this kind of defense because he had a relationship with my barrister outside of court that presumably revolved around golf greens and an old school tie. As improbable as this analysis appears it is even more impossible to find any other explanation for the way in which the trial was conducted. It was a case of invisible alliances, unstated obligations and obvious personal prejudice. It was so confusing that I was relieved when they took me down to the dungeons beneath the courts while they discussed my case in some legal language far too important for the ears of the accused.

I was escorted directly down from the dock and through a series of tunnels that looked like something out of the Count of Monte Christo. There were sideways shafts that led to derelict cells where skeletal remains from convict times might still have been chained to the walls. The tunnels were so low that you had to crouch. They might have been made for the convenience of the rats that were evident everywhere rather than for the sad human traffic that reluctantly shared their space. We finally came to a large opening where there were a series of holding cells where I deposited with the remand prisoners from Long Bay Prison. This was slightly disconcerting until I heard a familiar voice calling my name. Big Jim appeared from the mass of miscreants and was very pleased to see me. He laughed my fears away by saying he had told them that I was nowhere near the place and had nothing to do with it. He asked how everyone was and I told him the gossip. He said that they had warrants for him in three different states as well as back in New Zealand so he wouldn't be seeing anyone for quite a while. We were discussing what I should do with the few possessions that he had left at Stanmore when one of the warders realised that we were conferring and freaked out. It appears that by trying to scare me by putting me in with hardened criminals they had accidentally placed me in the perfect place to give me peace. There was a moment of pure panic before I was removed from the cell amidst much cursing and confusion. We waved goodbye for the last time as the other prisoners joked and jeered at the incompetence of our jailers. I was taken back upstairs to be told by the judge that he had directed the jury to deliver a verdict of not guilty due to lack of evidence and I was released as a free and very happy man.

As I left the courthouse with my parents we bumped into Ross and Andy Guerilla. I pogoed around them in celebration unable to control my jubilation which made my father furious. He later declared that I was never to see those people again and that the suit that I was wearing was now to be my new uniform. My mother had already burned all of the punk clothes that I had spent so many hours making. I knew that I had to escape and disappeared out the back window a few nights later. After walking all the way to Wentworthville Station I realised that there was a train strike and had to grab a cab all the way to Australia Street in Newtown. The house at Australia Street was occupied by Les Wreckage, Nick Sleaze, Greg Wino and Craig Jones. Craig had the ground floor room that was a former shop front and he agreed to share with me. Behind our bedroom was a small lounge area which led to a spacious kitchen and out to the backyard. The laundry and shower were out the back to the right and there were three bedrooms upstairs so we were all quite comfortable. The house at Stanmore had slowly filled up with garbage and had been ceremoniously ransacked in a Destroy Party where sections of the walls had been removed and taken away as souvenirs. The house at Australia Street was our home for a long time and survived many similar half-hearted attempts at destruction.

The closest that Australia Street came to actual destruction was during a three-day party that only lasted two days for reasons that will become obvious. The party began with the Brisbane band Razar playing in the shop front bedroom. Razar were a very tight outfit that had a single out called 'Task Force' about undercover Brisbane cops trying to infiltrate the punk scene. They had played at the Grand Hotel and stayed at the pub because they did not know anyone from Sydney. Razar were a great band and rocked the neighborhood. The neighbors stood outside on the street unsure whether to dance or call the cops. The evening ended in total debauchery and drunkenness with bodies strewn around the rooms like so many empty flagons. We woke up to a breakfast of acid and pot which was much better than the nothing that we usually had in the mornings. Someone put on the radio and we heard the news that some punks had been stabbed near Taylor Square which instantly killed the mood. Scotch Jim suggested that we ring our parents and let them know that we weren't the victims. Jim, Nick, Charley and I went down to the phone booth on a nearby corner. Jim was first in the booth while we hung outside. Then the acid addled our brains and bodies. Nick threw up straight away and Jim leant out of the phone box to tell us to move him around the corner when he started throwing up as well. It must have been contagious because pretty soon all four of us were vomiting and hallucinating and walking into walls. I can't remember if we managed to make the phone calls but we did manage to make it back to the house. We sat down just in time to witness Bailey come bouncing through the front doors with the two stabbing victims yelling 'guess who got stabbed' like some kind of macabre game show host.

One victim was Dave Armband who had had a knife thrust through his upper right lip. The cut went all the way up to the corner of his right eyeball and had taken a good piece of his nose on the way. He was lucky that he hadn't lost the eye. He had been stitched up so badly that a section of flesh near his nostril still looked like it was hanging loose. The other victim was Vic Vomit's friend Paul who had been slashed in an arch from the corner of his left eye to the corner of his left lip. The two cuts were so precise that they seemed like signatures and Dave and Paul told us that the language was Lebanese. This started a ridiculous racist reaction. Bailey started ranting and raving around the lounge room trying to organise a vigilante squad to go out and hunt down any wogs that they could find. This was so stupid because there was no chance of finding the actual culprits. Also, we were in the middle of Newtown which was full of working-class Italian and Greek families.

Everyone was getting so carried away that it seemed impossible to stop the stupidity so I dived on Charley and wrestled him to the ground. Charley knew that I was kidding but our pretence was so convincing that people started chanting fight! Fight! Fight! When it seemed that the excitement might cause an actual fight we separated and stood side by side shaking hands. I told them that if Bailey was serious about fighting wogs then he may as well start with Charley. Bailey backed down pretty quickly because Charley was like a chainsaw once he was started up and his fierce facial expression soon cut through the racist rubbish. The mood soon shifted from righteous anger to deep depression as people began to drown their dreams of revenge in alcohol. The atmosphere became so heavy and horrible that Charley and I decided to go to the cemetery over the road in order to get some fresh air and stop our trip from becoming a total downer. Once we were in the park we sat down and soaked up the healing rays of the sun. The elevation in our mood was almost instantaneous. We realised that we had an obligation to offer the same transcendent experience to every punk at the party and especially to those who were tripping. We set out on our secret mission from what we had decided to call 'happy land' determined to rescue the inhabitants of 'gloomy land' from despair. Even as we crossed the road from the park and turned the corner the day was turned from sunshine into shadow by the surrounding buildings. We felt like we were angels of light descending into darkness.

One by one we contacted the punks who were tripping and convinced them to come across the road. Some people proved hard to budge and did not believe in the curative powers of sunshine or the 'happy water' that we offered. Once we had talked them into crossing the road, they all quickly became converts and joined in our evangelical mission. Punks who had recently been consumed by despair and dark thoughts of revenge were now frolicking on the grass like a bunch of helpless, happy hippies. Nick proved the hardest to convince and sat on the back steps brooding, dismissing our claim that we had discovered paradise. Charley and I eventually had to pick him up and carry him across the road. He instantly saw the light and decided to go back to get his movie camera in order to capture this most magical mood. When he returned the movie camera became the fascination of Kiwi Kim. She firstly captured the camera and then became obsessed with a back yard that bordered the park which had been painted completely purple. Kim was so out of it that she was only capable of pressing the lens against the fence while mumbling 'it's so purple' over and over again. This is not to say that Kim was any madder than the rest of us but only that we had hit upon the perfect acid trip at the most imperfect time.

As the sun settled the police began patrolling the park and instituted an informal curfew. Anyone who was caught out on the street that did not live in the immediate vicinity was either being arrested or escorted down to Newtown train station. We only discovered this when Wino was caught travelling over to another punk house in Hordern Street where Laura Horizontal and Dell were living. He told the cops that he lived there so he wouldn't be arrested. He tried to sneak back to Australia Street with the girls but was stopped again. This time he told them that he lived in Australia Street. This was true but the cops recognized him and arrested him for lying. The police did not like arresting girls because there weren't many female officers in those days so they were much harder to handle. They also had to be housed in separate cells which cut down the available space and reduced their quota.

Hordern Street was also important because it was where Richard Rejex met his future bride. There were three English girls who had joined the scene. Two of them were attractive looking girls and one was not. Richard had paired up with a tall curly haired girl named Linda who later became our Yoko Ono. I was over there one night with Richard and Dave from Chaos. Dave disappeared into a bedroom with the second attractive girl which left me feeling rather uncomfortable with the third girl. I was pretty drunk but I wasn't blind. I did not want to insult the girl but I certainly did not want to sleep with her. We sat on the floor eyeing each other awkwardly for several minutes. I could not think of any easy way out until my savior appeared in the form of a big brown cockroach crawling along the carpet. Without thinking about the consequences, I picked it up and popped it right into my mouth. It was like chewing a hard-coated candy with a soft centre that tasted terrible. The pommy girl got up screaming and ran from the room. I got up and went home happy to have avoided hurting her feelings. The next morning, I got up to go to work at the Housing commission. Everything seemed normal as I caught the train into town. It was not until the train was pulling into Central station that my stomach started to rumble. The memory of legs and shell crumbling in my mouth added fuel to the fire. The doors on the train were the new electric ones and could not be opened manually. I swallowed several times and did my best to hold it in until we reached the station. As the doors opened my stomach exploded and vile vomit spewed forth. I must have lost half my body weight because it did not stop for several seconds. I was like a fire hose filled with fetid filth. The waiting workers jumped aside but none could escape the splash of the spew. None of these unfortunate commuters were going to work that day and I too retired home to lament my gallant but misguided gesture.

Meanwhile back at Australia Street the girls eventually got back to give us the bad news and we settled in for a siege. All of the tripping punks managed to barricade ourselves upstairs in Les' bedroom. We felt like we were under attack from the police and the rest of the depressed partygoer's downstairs. There was no electric light in Les' room so we lit candles and sat around in a circle like we were holding a séance. The only person who interrupted our peace was Animal who forced the door open in order to borrow Les' cutthroat razor. Mad Dog had decided to play party games with some of the young punks downstairs. The Hurstville boys had turned up belatedly with large plastic bottles filled with their infamous homemade slivovitz mixed with red cordial. Punks who were unfamiliar with the potion were unwittingly sculling the innocuous looking liquid and dropping like flies. The downstairs area resembled the set of a slasher film with bodies piled up everywhere with the rest of the partygoers wandering around like zombies. We could hear the mayhem being unleashed beneath us but chose to ignore it. We were the calm centre in the eye of the storm and remained that way until the police arrived.

Apparently, Bailey had finally gotten up the courage to confront someone somewhere and had escaped the house and the police blockade long enough to throw a brick through the front window of a neighbor's house. As there was a child sleeping in the front room and the police quite rightly got upset and decided to put a premature end to our three-day party. We watched out Les' window as partly sober punks were directed down the road towards the station while the very drunk ones were thrown into the back of bull wagons and taken to the cells for the night. The mayhem that they met on the ground floor could in no way have prepared them for the peace and love that was awaiting them upstairs. When they finally forced their way into Les' bedroom, we were still seated in our cosmic circle with our candles burning brightly. We greeted them politely and acted like the superior beings that we felt ourselves to be. We sympathised with the police assessment of our friends downstairs and elaborated on their description of them as useless drunken thugs. Whatever spell we had woven seemed to work as they politely questioned each one of us in turn to ascertain whether we lived there or not. One by one we replied that we did and were left alone until Charley for some silly reason said 'no' and they dragged him off kicking and screaming down the stairs. He probably would have gotten to go home if he hadn't stumbled as he walked out the door but the police threw him in the back of the van assuming that he was drunk. He was one of the few tripping punks to spend the night in the cells and it seemed like he had been sent straight into hell.

Everyone else soon left like rats deserting an already sunken ship. Les was so disgusted that he retired to the country for a few weeks. Craig went back to stay with his mum for a while and Wino was still in the lockup. Nick and I were the only residents left in residence with Kiwi Kim as the only remaining guest. The three of us sat amidst the devastation in the lounge room quietly staring into oblivion while one brave blowfly buzzed around our heads. It was as if Armageddon had finally arrived but had only hit our house. It was possibly the worst hangover of all time and only got worse as we slowly came down from the acid. Then Kiwi Kim remembered that she had stashed a bag of pot under Les' carpet when the cops had arrived. We raced each other up the stairs and soon recovered the pot and our cosmic calm as the medicinal properties of the holy herb blew away our blues.

Kim eventually left but thankfully left us the pot and Nick and I made a space amidst the wreckage to lie down and sleep. I was woken up to the strange sounds of what seemed to be people cleaning. I thought it must be magical elves and kept my eyes closed so that I did not disturb them. I thought that I recognised Fenton's voice amongst the predominantly female chatter but stayed still because it still seemed like a dream. When the house was finally quiet, I dared to open my eyes and saw that my dream had come true. The house was cleaner than it had ever been and even the fridge had been recovered from the backyard and reconnected. Nick was already awake and sitting in wonder in the lounge room drinking the tea that the kindly elves had left for us. We smoked pot and drank tea for breakfast and felt sorry for all those who had gone home and missed out on this most amazing of all the punk miracles. Sometimes the worst people can do the best things, life can be funny like that!

CHAPTER 9

It was around this time that the Sydney scene was invaded by North Shore punks. A gang of six or seven guys with slicked back hair who all dressed in black leather jackets and blue jeans like they were Fonzie impersonators. They were from an alien culture and behaved accordingly. They had heard the rumble of the drums in the jungle and had been attracted to the sound but had missed the message. They were a serious sub-group whose first loyalty was to each other rather than to the overall movement. One evening they entered the front bar of the Grand Hotel in a bad mood and had started hassling some lone punk at the bar. This was an aberration as punks never fought punks. I took exception to their behavior and told them that they were out of line. The head North Shore boy and the chief instigator was called Spen. He was well over six feet tall and was built like a front row forward. I was sixty kilos dripping wet and wasn't keen to take him on and I would also be contradicting my original assertion that punks didn't fight punks. He didn't care and would have started then and there but Fred stepped in with his bat from under the bar and told him to cool it. Spen didn't appreciate the intervention and told me that I was gutless. I told him that if he still wanted to fight me later, I would be happy to oblige him later that night at Frenches Tavern.

I stood in front of the stage at Frenches later that night happily dancing to whomever was playing. I had forgotten all about fighting until I was grabbed collared from behind and dragged towards the stairs. It took me some seconds to realise that it was Spen and the boys ready to rumble and there wasn't much that I could do about it. I was propelled up the stairs and out of the front door onto Oxford Street. I was wearing my bright red and orange pants with pink jacket. It must have looked like they were kidnapping a clown. When we got outside onto the street Spen and the boys manhandled me around the corner and down an alleyway. They were chattering constantly about how badly I was about to be beaten. From the way that things were going, I really had no grounds to disagree. There was no way that I was going to win against these numbers so I decided to try and even up the odds. I started telling Spen what a wimp he was needing a whole gang to take on one skinny punk. I told him that I was going to tell everyone that he was scared to take me on one on one so everyone would know what a coward he was. When we arrived at a suitable spot, I told him that if he was scared and couldn't face me by himself then he wasn't worth fighting anyway. Spen got so mad that he exploded at his mates, telling them all to get back around the corner and wait until he had finished with me. They didn't like leaving but Spen was so incensed that he was almost ready to begin bashing them. They reluctantly retreated around the corner snarling and spitting insults at me as they went.

We faced off like David and Goliath but without the sling. Spen told me that I could have the first punch because I was so small. I didn't wait for a second invitation and hit him as hard as I could up under the jaw hoping to get lucky and knock him out with one blow. I was never very lucky though and I only made him mad. I spent the next few minutes trying hard to stay inside and block his blows. Throwing occasional punches in between his haymakers which were blazing away right and left. It wasn't long before the boys were back. They expected the contest to be over and we had to pause in order to persuade them to give us a bit more time. Their impatience was matched by Spen's frustration and he had to turn his fury on his friends again before they would leave us alone. When we finally focused, I tackled him into a parked car. We proceeded to bang each other's heads against it until the owner came out and threatened to call the police.

The best thing about fighting big guys is that they tend to do the bear. This means that they get as big as they can in order to intimidate their opponent. They tend to spread their arms out wide and swing wide as well. This leaves a lot of room up the middle to target the face and chin if you can dodge the punches. The other advantage of being shorter than your opponent is that you can use your legs for leverage in order to get extra power into your punches. Despite these obvious advantages I still didn't have the punching power to knock him out. I had to rely on throwing a lot of punches aimed at the eyes in order to blind him and distract him rather than doing any actual damage. Despite the genius of my strategy he did manage to hit me hard and often and it was only the hardness of my head that kept me in the contest. Spen's friends kept coming around the corner every five minutes to check on our progress. Spen kept breaking off the fight to chase back around the corner. At one point they got so frustrated that I thought they were about to start fighting each other but each time his friends would retreat and we would start all over again.

They eventually came back and said that we had been fighting for forty minutes. I was so exhausted by this stage that I could hardly stand. I told myself that if I felt that bad then he was probably feeling worse. This is the other advantage of fighting big guys. If you can't knock them out you might be able to wear them out. His friends left us alone and we faced off in the alley one more time too tired to even trade insults. I then remembered the sage advice of Johnny Dole, that there were no rules in a street fight. I kicked him in the balls as hard as I could and dropped him to his knees. I kicked him in the face and pinned him to the ground. I did not have the strength to hit him or even lift my arms so I grabbed his hair and started banging his head on the road. Spen eventually stopped struggling so I rolled off him and lent against a parked car. It wasn't long before his friends came back around the corner again. I dragged Spen up against the car so he didn't look dead and we waited patiently in in a pool of blood. Spen friends dragged him to his feet. They were reluctant to take him home to his mother covered in blood. I told them that they could come back to my house if they wanted and clean him up first. They still insisted on wanting to know who won even though it was pretty obvious that there was no winner in this particular contest. I told them it was a draw because Spen was still having a hard time speaking. We went up the alley together to buy a flagon of scrumpies from Frenches and then all went back to my place in South Dowling Street to get clean and drunk.

The fight broke the resolve of the North Shore punks when it came to trying to take over the punk scene. I saw one of Spens' friends years later at the Trade Union Club and he asked me how I had finished up. I told him that I had gone to work the next day at the Housing Commission where some wag had said 'should see the other guy'. I know I must have looked like a mess but having to bite my tongue didn't help. He told me that Spen had spent the next week in bed being fed through a straw by his mother. I'm sure that the damage done to his ego was far worse than that done to his body. The trouble with being a bully and constructing your whole persona around being terrifying and indestructible is that the entire construct crumbles once the bully is beaten. I hope that Spen recovered fully and went on to live a happy life. It was never my intention to destroy him but only to stop him from destroying me. Spens' friend finished by saying that he thought that I had won the fight but I told him that there were no winners when punks fought punks.

CHAPTER 10

Punk hit the big time when we arrived at Rags sometime in seventy-nine. Rags was the refurbished Chequers Nightclub on Goulburn street. It had hosted big bands and big acts from here and overseas in the Fifties and Sixties. Rags was entered via a flight of stairs that ended in a small foyer. The foyer was patrolled by Terry the doorman. Terry had been around longer than anyone. He had come up from Melbourne with Mick Cox and Ian Riland from Rose Tattoo. He had worked as a bouncer since the late sixties. His last job had been doing the door at the Bondi Lifesaver solo. He never wasted a punch and had the fastest hands I've ever seen. He was just over seventy kilos in those days but hit like a heavyweight. He used to work clubs in the Cross alone that would have had three blokes working if he hadn't been there. Terry let everyone in for free once he knew who we were. Once you got passed Terry you went through double doors onto a section of floor that was slightly raised. This extended down passed the bar on the left to the toilets and pinball machines at the back. The raised area also extended around the sides of the huge wooden dance floor. This area was lined with individual booths and upholstered seating that would have suited the celebrity guests of the sixties but was far too plush for punks. The stage stood opposite the bar and took up almost the entire back wall. There was a passage stage right that led to the alleyway at the back of the venue for loading gear. There was also a small dressing room with old style makeup mirrors stage left.

Why the management would invite punks into such a large and luxurious space was a bit of a mystery. We had been invited there for an industry event featuring an almost punk band called The Press. The band was related to the hoodlums who ran the club and were older and hairier than most punks. They dressed in mock military gear and were a really good Rock n' Roll band that had somehow lost their way and decided upon Punk as a possible path to success. That the Press needed an audience as well as support bands was the obvious explanation. That it was being used as a tax dodge and a means of laundering large amounts of money was less obvious but probably more meaningful. The best thing about our new organized crime connections was that they were also connected to the police. There was no criminal activity in Sydney in the seventies that did not have police protection. This meant that we were never raided at Rags like we were at the Grand. There were occasional incursions by undercover cops but this was only to gain intelligence because the police didn't have any. We were so pleased with the place that we didn't quibble over explanations and soon made Rags our new home.

Undercover infiltration proved difficult for the police because there were height and weight restrictions in the force in those days. They all looked like front row forwards and stood out in a room full of skinny kids. They would come into the venue and stand sheepishly on the dance floor hoping not to be noticed. They would then copy the dance style of whomever they happened to see first. The most obvious and most easily imitated dance style was that of Dancing Dez. he was no longer around but had left his legacy in the form of students of his style like Laura Horizontal and Robbo the yobbo. The dance style was so unique and familiar to us that anyone imitating it instantly became obvious. It was such a source of amusement in the scene that I penned a song in their honour entitled 'Pig fat, pig fat, sizzling in the ruins' which was about blowing up a police station. It was a sing-a-long song and I would jump from the stage and present the microphone to one of these conspicuous impersonators in order to get them to sing the chorus which always brought a huge cheer from the crowd.

Rags was a safe haven but the Grand Hotel was still fair game for the cops. One night we walked out of the Grand to find the whole road outside the pub lined by police cars and bull wagons. We waited outside on the footpath until everyone had left the venue because there was always safety in numbers. After some discussion we decided to stick together and try it to make to Rags. We started slowly up George Street not saying or doing anything that would give them an excuse to exercise their authority. Rod Rodent soon took the lead and led us up George Street like the pied piper dancing a jig. He seemed totally unconcerned and cavorted his way up the road waving at the cops like they were our escorts rather than our enemies. As we moved up the street the police moved with us in a long convey of vehicles. They seemed intent on keeping us on the left-hand side of the road. Some punks got nervous and decided to make a break for it but the police jumped from their cars and herded them into the back of a bull wagon. We had never been confronted with such a large and well organised police presence. These were brand new tactics that they must have spent hours in the squad room planning. We felt like we were caught in a trap. We had gotten about half way up the hill and were just approaching the intersection of Golbourn Street. This signaled our escape point to Rags and punks began to panic. Just when we were about to lose our collective faith entirely Rod turned left towards China Town. This was the opposite direction to where we wanted to go. As we had little choice, we all chose to follow Rod. We were half way down the wrong way street with all the cop cars close beside us when Rod spun around suddenly and sprinted back up the hill towards George Street.

It was only then that the brilliance of Rods' strategy became apparent. The police convoy had followed us into a much smaller and heavily congested one-way street. There was traffic in front of them and behind them which made it impossible to maneuver. Several police cars tried to back up but that only made matters worse. Some turned on their sirens but this only added to the confusion. Police began to panic and started jumping from their vehicles but their organisation and communication were shot to pieces. Punks were running up the bonnets and over the rooves of their cars. Others were having their car doors slammed in their faces as they tried to extricate themselves from their vehicles. The police were now facing a punk stampede. Songs were sung and bums were bared as we ran across George Street and all the way to Rags. Once we were there, we knew that we were safe when we witnessed Terry the doorman's welcoming smile.

The worst thing about Rags was that it was inconveniently located just up the road from a disco called Studs. The pathetic patrons of this establishment used to hang out on the footpath of an evening waiting for girls who never appeared. This sad social situation and the fact that their music came from pieces of plastic fueled their frustration. They tended to take out this frustration on any unwitting passersby especially punks. Their ridiculous random acts of violence led to an all-out street war that went on for several months. A solitary stud did come into Rags once in order to inform us that they were all former Town Hall Sharps so we should simply surrender. Rod Rodent then began to question him about his former acquaintances in such a friendly and familiar manner that the guy became quite embarrassed. Rod mentioned several ex-sharps by name and enquired about their health and what they were doing now. The guy became quite agitated and stumbled and stammered and it soon became obvious that his bluff had been called. The longer the conversation went the more obvious and hilarious the situation became. Everyone managed to keep calm and enjoy the encounter as a performance piece. Raucous laughter did not ensue until the stammering stud left with his tail between his legs. The conversation demonstrated both Rods' reputation as an arch mind manipulator and the enduring reputation of the Town Hall Sharps.

The attacks against punks on their way up from The Grand Hotel became so prevalent that we started travelling in packs for protection. When a punk was taken it became routine for their friends to run up to Rags and raise the alarm rather than fight on the spot. Once the alarm was raised punks would come pouring out of the place and down the road like a stampede of serious psychosis. Confronted by sheer numbers the studs would usually release whomever they had captured and both gangs would retreat to their respective establishments. Such circumstances became so common that when Rejex were playing punks would come straight to the stage when someone was attacked so that the announcement could be made directly over the P.A. system. I remember stopping one of our biggest gigs in order to jump off the stage and lead the counter attack. The deadly drama of a street fight was always much more entertaining than a mere musical punk performance. Those who were not used to our regular rumbles would stand amazed as all the punks in the room would drain out like a toilet had been flushed. The unaccustomed customers would be left standing in an almost empty venue until we returned triumphantly several minutes later celebrating the rescue of some poor punk who was usually bloody from being badly beaten.

As the rumbles became routine the studs started chasing us back up the hill after we had completed our rescue missions and would be pelted with bottles by whatever punks had remained behind. The studs retaliated by pelting us with bottles as we ran down to rescue our friends. This became a regular part of the game and the collection of suitable projectiles was like a part time job for some punks. Sometimes these skirmishes escalated into major scuffles but our mission was always search and rescue rather than search and destroy. Sometimes the studs would follow us down the stairs of Rags once we had completed our rescue and Terry would punch them back up the stairs again. It didn't matter how many studs there were none of them ever made it through the double doors into the venue. Terry still complains about the lack of support he received on these occasions and I still tell him to stop whining because that was his job!

Although no one was badly injured one person was killed as a result of this ongoing turf war. One night some stud decided to sneak in through the back entrance of Rags and steal some musical equipment. The thieves had failed to disclose the plan to all of their friends. Some of them had decided to lie in wait with a gun across the alley from the same exit waiting for unsuspecting punks. The intervening alleyway was not well lit so when the guys with the gun saw people exiting with musical equipment they shot and killed one of their own. The shooting was one of two incidents that made the newspapers in a major way while we were at Rags. The second was a street fight that involved about a hundred people on each side. The bands had just finished performing on this particular night when someone came in with the news that the Studs boys were outside waiting for us in large numbers. They were reported to be heavily armed with clubs and knives. This meant that we had two major problems. The first one being that, unlike the Studs, we had a large number of females that needed protection. The second was that we did not carry weapons and had no way of obtaining them on such short notice. Conferences were held and panic held at bay as we decided upon our exit strategy. We were going to let the girls go out the back while we distracted the Studs at the front but realised that the back exit was also being watched. The fact that someone had been shot exiting that way recently meant that it probably wasn't the best option. We then decided to gather everyone together on the stairs and form a guard around the more vulnerable members. With all of the females in the middle of the group we walk out of the doors and make our way as quickly as we could up to Pit Street. We would then try to stay in formation all the way to the Stage Door Tavern which was only about a hundred yards away down the hill.

When we were ready and revved up, we burst out the door and started up the road and around the corner. We went at a steady pace so that no girls were exposed and even the pill heads could keep up. We got most of the way down Pit Street and almost to the corner of Campbell Street before our formation fell apart. The opposition had caught up and had grabbed someone from the back of our group. Like frightened sheep the mob of punks panicked and bolted mindlessly down the hill. The girls began screaming and it became impossible to communicate. No one at the front of the group knew what was happening at the back. We all ran to the corner on the opposite side of the road before distance gave us some perspective. We realised that the opposition were not in pursuit but were instead busy bashing the one lone punk that they had managed to grab.

Scotch Jim, Wino and I stood on the corner grabbing passing punks hoping to gather enough numbers for a counter attack. Someone stopped long enough to tell us that Animal had not liked the idea of running and had turned to take on the mob alone. All we could see from the corner was a mass of bodies surrounding something on the ground like sharks in a feeding frenzy. We managed to stop a few punks from fleeing and regrouped on the corner before charging back across the road into the backs of our enemy. I remember running across the road screaming as loudly as I could. There were so many of them that I decided to leap in the air Kung Fu style. I was hoping to make a hole that the following punks could get through in order to rescue our fallen comrade. I missed everyone and hit the ground hard. I covered up and waited for the kicking to commence. After several seconds I was surprised to find that I had received no boots to the head. I got to my feet and was faced by two young boys holding pocketknives. They looked really nervous and ready to run. I made a feint towards one and he fled in panic with his friend following close behind. As I looked up and down the road it became obvious that we were not fighting studs but a random ragtag army of street kids and miscellaneous miscreants. They were led by an indigenous guy who had frequented the scene for a short time. He must have scoured the block in Redfern and the surrounding city to get this gang together. The fight was spread out all over the entire intersection. I remember seeing Big Mick swinging a wooden bus stop around his head like a bat and Mick Lips throwing some kid through a shop front window. Terry the Doorman then came down the road like the cavalry and the tide soon turned in our favour. A lot of punks had come back from the Stage Door once the girls were safely secured and joined in the fight. The remnants of the ragtag army that we were facing soon fled into the night and we were free to go the Stage Door to celebrate. The newspapers the next day wrote of how several hundred gang members had fought it out on Sydney's streets. It was certainly the biggest brawl that punks were ever involved in but there were never the numbers that the papers claimed and I never even threw a punch.

It in the early days of Rags that I sacked Stuart the drummer. He had missed a rehearsal and told me that a brick had fallen on his head at the building site where he worked. The lameness of the excuse was precisely the excuse I had been looking for and his timing had never been better. We played a couple of gigs with John Blood from Melbourne but soon found a human metronome in the form of Don Ego. Don was a naïve boy from somewhere near Campsie in Sydney's south. He got his name by being overly obsessive with his appearance. He would have the rear vision mirror in his car fixed permanently towards his face and would snip his spiked hair while driving until it was all exactly the same length. He once introduced me to a girl he had met and told me that she was his girlfriend even though she was obviously a prostitute. He stormed off in a rage when I told him what I thought of her but soon came back repentant when her pimp punched him out outside her hotel in the Cross one night. Don had no sense except for his sense of timing and helped transform the band from a second-rate support act into second rate headliners.

I remember the first time that we played at Rags on the big stage with a proper P.A. and a light show I was so terrified that I lost my voice. I walked around the venue before the gig whispering in people's ears asking how I was supposed to sing if I couldn't even talk? I walked out onto the stage and stood in front of the microphone totally unsure of what was about to happen. I listened to Richard, Nick and Don start up the song without sharing any of the energy and anticipation that had marked our performances at the Grand Hotel. When I heard the cue to sing my voice exploded and the fold-back was so loud that it almost knocked me over. I hadn't regained my nerve but had lost my sense of self and went into that semi-conscious state that marks the miracle of the muse as your ego is washed away by the creative tide.

It was also around this time, whatever time this was, that Rejex and Suicide Squad were approached by Roger Thought Criminal to record singles for his new label Doublethink. Rejex turned up at the recording school at the bottom of Devonshire Street near Central Station in Richard's big yellow van. We were still discussing which songs to record on the way there. We eventually decided upon 'Who Wants to March When You Can Riot' which was our most popular live song. Who Wants to March had been inspired by the arrival of the Brisbane punks and their unpunk propensity to take part in organized marches against the law in Queensland forbidding marching. Niagara Baby was chosen for the B side. The lyrics were written after I had seen a big, fat, cigar smoking executive explaining away the birth defects caused by toxic chemicals buried at Love Canal which was a suburb near Niagara Falls. The cynical attitude of the executive and the romantic irony of the location were too powerful to ignore. The juxtaposition seemed to sum up everything that we would have rebelled against if we could have been bothered. We also put the riff from Eskyland on the end so only people who had seen us live would get the joke.

The engineer was not a paid professional but was a friend of Rogers who was studying at the studio and had to record something as part of his course requirements. It was a very strange and uncomfortable experience because the band was used to taking their cues from me. They relied on my vocals and dancing in order to know when to do the changes. It took them sometime to learn how to count the bars. They still needed me to stand in the room and conduct them with movements and mime before they could get everything right. It was even harder for me because I had never sung while listening to myself sing. My whole musical experience had been about being overwhelmed by a wave of sound that filled me with the energy and enthusiasm necessary to perform. Roger kept telling me to sing like I did when I sang live but this was impossible because we were not live and it proved impossible to pretend. The end result was a tame and nervous reflection of the real Rejex but was still some way better than bad. We were just glad to have recorded something and did not particularly care whether the finished product was professional. Suicide Squad recorded their single at the same place and at around the same time. Mark Suicide's little sister wrote the lyrics for 'I Hate School' and it shows. I believe that Annie wrote the lyrics for New Kids Army and as far as I know Mark wrote the music for both. The two singles started Roger's business career and he is still the only person from the Sydney scene to have made any money from Punk. Fortunately, we were not into making money, we were into making mischief.

Rags saw the turning of the tide for the punk movement as it changed from a private club into a growing public concern. On some nights at Rags the straight crowd would outnumber the punks. We had covered the city in Rejex posters where bands had previously relied on word of mouth. We made these posters for free at a C.Y.S.S office in the Cross. Ironically, this was part of a government program to keep kids off the streets. We even put posters on the entrance to the Harbour Bridge and a number of kids from the northern suburbs turned up. I only knew this because I saw an ex-girlfriend of mine from Pymble in the audience. I went to talk to her after the gig but she ran away because she was terrified. Visiting a punk venue for some people was akin to upper class people touring Bedlam asylum in the last century. It was the thrill of expectant danger and the smell of the theatre of violence that attracted them. The venue was close to full on most nights that we played but not as full as when the Urban Guerillas played their final farewell performances. The Guerillas had been around for a long time by then and had made many friends. Andy and Ross were popular people and many old friends from Glen Innes as well as the city came to wish them well. These were without doubt the biggest punk audiences that ever happened in Sydney and the Guerillas deserved all of the accolades that they received. Short Bob was long gone but Danny Rumour was not a bad replacement and Rags went off on the six or seven occasions that they performed their last ever gig. It was a shame to see them go and signaled the end of the golden age of punk music in the Sydney scene just as the punk population was reaching its peak. Sometimes you go searching for something when the something you seek is right under your feet, life can be funny like that!

CHAPTER 11

Rags may have signaled the pinnacle of Punk but the best band to play there was not a punk band at all. Seems Twice were a trio from somewhere in Sydney's southern suburbs who played without fanfare or familiarity on several occasions. They had a set that ran about forty minutes with songs that only lasted about forty seconds. They were tight and talented and did not pause for breath in between numbers. They pumped out an endless stream of pop classics that were all similar but different with the same excessive exuberance. Some songs would last a matter of seconds which kept everyone guessing by arousing and defying expectations all at the same time. Punks may have been parochial but they were not stupid. Any act with quality and originality was applauded regardless of cultural affiliations.

The venue also played host to a number of mainstream bands. Australian Crawl played there early in their career. This was just before they appeared on Countdown. The singer had been in a motorcycle accident and had both of his arms in plaster. Cathi Corpse thought that this was funny and made everyone appreciate her point of view by moving the microphone stand sideways while the band was playing. The movement was not enough to stop the song but just enough to make things difficult. The singer would have to move just a foot to the left or right each time. He tried to maintain his professionalism by pretending that nothing was happening. This only exaggerated the hilarity of the whole situation. When the first song finished there was a standing ovation. The band seemed uncertain whether it was sincere as Cathi stood before them on the dance floor elaborately accepting our applause.

Pommy Ian copied Cathi's performance when the Ted Mulray Gang played. Ted could not control the mike stand because he also played the bass. Cathi and Ian were both into downers. Their pill head performances were made even more amazing because they could hardly stand up. Their exquisite timing was a miracle in itself. It was like watching Charley Chaplin doing his drunk routine. Ian's performance was made even more humorous as we made the band play 'Come jump in my car' over and over again. Ian enforced the song selection by moving the microphone away if they attempted to play anything else. The bands never saw the humour in these situations. Their search for stardom made them much too serious. This was the perfect punk performance demonstrating that if you didn't get the joke you were the joke!

The marathon music and movie days also became a feature at Rags. Inner-city artist Toby Zoates had filmed a number of performances at the Grand Hotel. These included a tour of the premises while Rejex were playing 'Who Wants to march!' as well as the Last Words playing to a packed punk house. He had also obtained obscure video clips of English punk bands like 999. A huge hushed house would sit in silence watching ourselves perform the punk ritual. This was like an out of body experience. Toby was also a renowned sound surfer. He would often stand in front of the stage with his eyes shut riding the sound waves. He would be totally oblivious to his surroundings and everyone would respect his space. Toby is still a transcendent artist and human being.

The marathon music days started sometime in the afternoon and seemed to last until no one was left standing. They also seemed to occur on scorching summer days. Although this may only have seemed so because the venue would become a sauna after a few hours. These days were so completely numbing to both mind and body that I find it impossible to remember who played. All I remember is a constant stream of punks wandering from Rags to the Civic Hotel across the road in order to buy cheaper beer. The early start meant that people were passing out all over the place by early evening. They were trials of endurance for everyone involved. The only antidote was speed and speed was in short supply in those days. After a few hours we had descended into a level of hell that even Dante could not have imagined. Ironically, the venue is still a sauna and 'massage parlour' and is still called Chequers. A different level of hell perhaps but hopefully much more pleasant.

Another memorable performance at Rags was by the Melbourne band Berlin. They were formed from the remnants of James Freud and the Teenage Radio Stars who had been loosely associated with Punk in the early days. They had played the night before at Frenches Tavern to an audience that was made up almost entirely of punks. Their arrogant attitude and rock star antics soon earned them the ire of the audience and spit soon hit the stage like a storm. Sydney punks did not spit often and certainly never at their own bands but Berlin were so serious about themselves that they left us little alternative. James Freud was so incensed that he jumped off the stage and tried to start a fight. Scotch Jim got him in a bear hug and paraded him around the room so that punks could spit on him directly. The guitar player also jumped into the crowd in order to rescue the singer. He was overwhelmed up by sheer numbers and was forced to retreat to the relative safety of the stage. Their bravery was rewarded by a cessation of spitting. The singer was eventually thrown bodily back onto the stage and they were allowed to finish their performance without any further fun.

The following evening Berlin were putting on their makeup in the band room at Rags. Super self-confidence and hairspray filled the air. I stood in the doorway for several seconds before they finally turned around and recognized me and my band. It must have seemed like a recurring nightmare and they recoiled suitably stunned and stupefied. James Freud jumped from his seat and demanded to know what we were doing there. He threatened to call the police and have us all thrown out. This was hilarious and we allowed him to rave for a while before informing him that we were the support band. The sheer terror took away their swagger and James slumped back into his seat. The arrogance that had characterised their performance on the previous night was gone. They took the stage without any rock star antics. With nothing but their musicianship to rely on they soon started to play without pretence. As they gave up their attitude and accepted the situation the audience accepted them. They escaped the volley of spit that had greeted them at Frenches. They were a good rock n' roll band when they weren't being wankers. The gig culminated in the guitar player being carried around the room on the shoulders of some punks and a great night was had by all.

Rose Tattoo also played at Rags. We had been to see them a few times. One night we went to see them at the Hordern Pavilion when there was almost no one there. It was weird to stand in the middle of that huge hall with all that loud music and nobody there to hear it. It was also amazing that many of the bands who had been on television could not pull a crowd in the city. It was the same when the Tatts played at Rags. This was when they had just returned from overseas. Rockin' Rob had replaced Mick Cox because Mick preferred partying to playing. There were the usual hard-core punters. Guys who were so insane that they would stick their heads in the bass bins. If their brains weren't rattled before they definitely had a screw loose afterwards. I remember Roger Thought Criminal standing next to me saying 'pick a few cords lay a few bricks' because he was an intellectual delinquent. The band was so loud that it proved impossible for the punks to stay in the room for more than a few minutes. By the time they were finished all the punks were hanging with Terry out in the foyer. I was tripping at the time and my ears were ringing in what seemed like some weird sonic celebration. The doors to the venue then burst open and Rod the Rat came through them holding Angry Anderson by the ear. He then dragged him up the stairs saying 'come on angry your mother wants you.' This was a weird. Not only was Angry a rock star he was also believed to be tough. Rose Tattoo had such a bad boy biker image that we had considered them untouchable. It was truly a moment when the whole world seemed to have turned upside down.

The world did turn upside down when there was a performance at Rags by a Melbourne band called Whirlywirl. The punk population was elsewhere early in the evening, busy tripping and performing random feats of mischief somewhere in the city. Someone had turned up with the trimmings from an acid blotter. The trips were called purple dreamers. It provided the most hallucinogenic experience that I have ever had. I remember returning to Rags and being confronted by the weirdest looking people that I had ever encountered. There was an abundance of fluorescent wigs, flowing gowns, burlesque style bodices and more bald heads covered in glitter than at a modern-day Mardi gras. It was a totally alien experience, like being at a circus on mars. The visual eccentricity was much more dramatic than anything concocted by punks or drag queens previously. We were overwhelmed and sat around the sides of the venue without trying to impress our presence on the performance at all. The music was as almost as wild as the costumes. There was a lot of electronic synthesized sound long before such things were popular. I remember sitting in one of the booths to the side of the dance floor and watching the wallpaper melt. This was something I had heard of happening in the folklore of the sixties but never experienced. The acid no doubt exaggerated the whole experience but it was certainly a trip well worth remembering.

The industry nights at Rags also included industry days. Record executives and agents were invited to come and see some new band or reassess an old one. There was a band called Little Ashley and the Incurables that used to play at Rags all the time without a following and whose very existence seemed to depend on these industry functions. Rejex were often asked to perform on these occasions although this was more to make sure that people turned up rather than to enhance our chances at a record deal. Sherbet were there on one such occasion after failing badly on a tour to the States and changing their name to Sherbs. Playing on such occasions demonstrated the difference between ritual and spectacle. The ritual only has true potency when performed as a part of a believing congregation. Once the ritual is removed from its cultural context it becomes a novelty act. Imagine a native Australian corroboree being performed on country, in a tribal setting where everyone participates and understands the significance of the performance. Then imagine this same ritual being performed on a city street in front of an audience of suits and strangers. This is when ritual changes into spectacle. The industry days at Rags provided the setting for such a change in dynamic. We were like priests performing a mass in front of atheists and were totally out of place. The members of Sherbs would have felt just as out of place and awkward at a punk party and we regarded each other with mutual disdain. The ritual was altered at Rags by both the industries involvement and by the imposition of the stage and footlights. Where everyone had previously been friends and had related to one another as equals some punks were now strangers and approached you as if you were some kind of celebrity if you played in a band.

The change in the ritual came with the change in venue but also through a change in the audience. The sheer size of Rags, along with our extensive advertising campaign, meant that many people came to gigs who wouldn't normally venture into such places. Mel Gibson was supposedly there while filming Mad Max. Frightened T.V personalities and aspiring actors would sometimes attend. We did not welcome such intrusions but it did provide us with an opportunity to perform even if it was only to display our displeasure. This was a contradiction within the culture because we wanted the attention but spat in the faces of those who dared to look. I was given ample opportunity to display my displeasure and on one night in particular when a gaggle of glamorous young things became brave enough to venture into our lair. When they asked at the bar for someone to show them around, I was happy to take on the job. They thought it was all very exciting and acted like they were on a lion safari as they clutched each other nervously and giggled incessantly. After a short time, the novelty began to wear thin. They had obviously been expecting mass murder or human sacrifice. After I had shown them the toilets and the pinball machines, they began to express their disappointment more openly. One of their male companions started to voice his boredom in such a caustic and condescending manner that I felt compelled to punch him in the head. This was not a full-blooded king hit referred to nowadays as a coward's punch. This was what was referred to as a love tap. A gentle poke in the nose to reprimand a person rather than injure them. His eyes went to water and he held his face in such shock that the girls started screaming hysterically. They eventually gathered their wits and ran from the venue in sheer panic. I was not happy that I hit him but I would have felt worse if they had gone away disappointed.

Rags also saw the appearance of two bands that signaled a schism in the punk culture. The first band was the Bedhogs who were formed by Danny Rumour in order to give his brother Jimmy a gig. Jimmy had been missing from the scene for some time. He had been diagnosed with lymphoma while playing with Black Runner. The doctors had decided that he was at deaths' door. People had visited him in Sydney hospital and smuggled him drugs to help him deal with death. He was on so much prescription medication at the time that it probably made little difference. He had lost a lot of weight and his hair had fallen out from the chemotherapy but Jimmy had kept his cool. No one questioned his miraculous return and Jimmy didn't like to talk about it. The other rising star to join the Bedhogs was Chris Cross. Chris had never played bass outside of his bedroom. He had to sit down in order to play but this just made him appear more punk. Danny did not really want to invest a great deal of time into the Bedhogs. He had another project that was more important to him at the time so he soon handed over the guitar playing duties to Mark Suicide Squad. Danny also recruited Don Ego from Rejex. Don told me that he was leaving the band while I was playing pinball. He was surprised to find that I was not upset and that I thought it was funny. Don wanted to be a rock star and had never really got the joke. Little Stewart also made his first appearance in a band with the Bedhogs when he joined them later on second guitar. No one seemed to know how Little Stewart got into the band. Mark assumed that Jimmy had invited him and Jimmy thought that Mark had done the same. By the time they realised that Stewart had invited himself he was already on the stage and had been playing with them for some time. The Bedhogs became the first punk supergroup.

Danny's other musical project was surrounded by so much secrecy that the original name was changed from the Ugly Mirrors to Sekret Sekret. I do not remember there being such interest generated around the formation of an inner-city band before. It was like the orchestrated hype preceding the release of a b-grade blockbuster. They were deliberately designed for commercial success. Like the Bedhogs this band also had the personnel for a punk super group but they were definitely not Punk. David Virgin had given up playing the bass in order to be the full-time front man. Andy Groom's brother Des took up the bass and a new guy on the scene named Slim Jim played the drums. The role of rhythm guitar was perfectly performed by Peter Perfect from the Scabs. They manufactured a kind of sixties retro chic as their image. They wore tight jeans and paisley shirts with oil lights as a backdrop. They also adopted an attitude of condescending cool. The Church later copied the concept and made a lot of money. The collective cool of Sekret Sekret could not disguise the fact that they were cute and poppy. They were like the love child of the Velvet Underground and the Bay City Rollers.

Sekret Sekret alienated the main body of the punk population while attracting a mostly female following. The good-looking girls from the early punk scene including Kirsty, Jenny and Robyn joined the kitsch cult. They were like the Manson family without the murder or the mayhem. They formed an elitist clique and waited for the feeding frenzy of fame to follow. Sekret Sekret did play some really good gigs because the musicianship was magical. They put out a single called New King Jack which had a nonsensical lyric with a killer guitar solo. Some members of the band then decided to add heroin chic to their mystique in order to celebrate their impending celebrity. The moment of truth came when they made their television debut on Donny Sutherland's Sounds one morning. It was their five minutes of fame but they froze in front of the cameras and retired to an ashram in order to recover.

CHAPTER 12

The Grand Hotel soon closed its doors for almost the last time. It had been a great pub and a great venue for many years. It was a home to many and undoubtedly the birthplace of Punk Rock in Sydney. It was to be refurbished and eventually reborn as a yuppie sandwich bar that was all black and white tiles and sterile steel. The band room became a bistro that failed to attract any business. We still went there occasionally to have a beer and reminisce. Because, as Little Rob said, 'you might not be able to live in the past but at least you can drink there.' Now you can't even do that.

The Civic Hotel soon took up the slack as another unwitting publican weighed the profit of a hundred ready patrons over the destructive power of Punk. The Civic Hotel was a toilet with a bar down one side. It was all tiles and steel and designed so that the blood and beer and urine could be hosed out after a hard night of drinking and brawling. Most Sydney hotels were designed in this way in the old days. Everyone would have thought that you were mad if you put carpet in a pub before the yuppies came to town. The place was run by a rundown old battle-axe named Meg. Meg became a surrogate mother to some of the girls in the scene. They would put in money on Mother's Day to buy her a present. Meg was a business woman who was happy to accept their affection as long as there was money attached. A rough headed, hard man named Ron worked the bar and kept the peace. He had beer for breakfast and seemed to sweat pure alcohol. He shared Fred's receding hairline and beer belly but lacked his diplomatic skills and sense of humour.

The bands played in a room upstairs that had been previously used for functions and parties. You entered through double doors at the back into a space very similar to the band room at the Grand. The major differences being that there was stage at the front and to the right and an L-shaped extension to the left. This was where tables were set and food could be served. The kitchen was at the back behind a small serving bench. There was no food at first because regulations did not insist on it at the time. When the regulations were changed and they were forced to sell food was finally served they should have changed the regulations again because the food was so awful. The band room had been dominated in previous years by Mat Finnish and Flowers. Mat Finnish were a great middle of the road rock band who never quite made it onto Countdown despite having a very large and loyal following. Flowers shamefully played Sex Pistols covers while only considering the cash and not the culture. We did see them play in the early days but they were so boring I can't really comment. It took quite a while for Meg to allow punk bands to play upstairs. For the first year or so we were quarantined to the downstairs bar. We did not mind as Rags had a much larger room and a much better stage for the musical aspect of our performance.

The scene was now divided between old punks and young punks. Old punks were veterans of the Grand hotel. Young punks were the sons and daughters of the Civic. The terms were a simple way to describe people because there were now so many punks. It was always difficult to differentiate individuals in the punk scene. The skinny, pale, kid with spiked hair and black jeans wasn't helpful. The young punks started to form new bands. Pommy Mark formed Positive Hatred with his brother Julian and Neil Ant on drums. Karl Buzzcock, who looked like a dayglo spaceman, formed Dogbox. There was also a band called Anti Hierarchy. And, just to show how far the scene had come since the days of the Last Resort, there was a band called World War 24. There was also a kid named Eager Penis who did not form a band but would later become a central figure in the Sydney scene. He earned his nickname from a nasty habit of trying to have sex with crashed out chicks at parties.

The Civic was a transit lounge from which we would launch our adventures and was hardly ever a place where adventures would actually happen. Punks would prepare themselves with drugs and alcohol and sit on the hard stools waiting for inspiration to strike. On one such night when nothing much was happening except for an excess of acid Rod Rodent and Chris Cross approached a bunch of us at the bar. They were full of mischief and promised us that the perfect party was happening somewhere in Surry Hills. Those of us who knew the terrible twins well were skeptical but their energy was always contagious. Chris could always charm the girls and Rod could con anyone so we were soon off our stools and on our way. The terrible twins made a terrific team and it was not long before we were dancing and singing and clowning our way up the hill to Irish town.

The first party that we arrived at was filled with suits and the smell of stale wine and cheap cheese. Rod stopped us at the door admitting that the prospects looked poor while also assuring us that there was a perfect party and it was happening just up the road. This set the scene for the rest of the night. Each disappointing party was followed by Rod promising that this was just an aperitif and the perfect party was not far away. When we doubted Chris Cross would chime in with his perfect patter about the perfect party. It seemed that the terrible twins had decided to take our tripping heads on a trip to nowhere purely for their own amusement. Each time we came across the semblance of a party it seemed so similar to the first one that it was like we were going around in circles. The skeptics began to protest and to rebel. We started urging the girls to go back to the Civic. Rod assured them that these parties were only a prelude and that he would now take us to the real perfect party.

After a few more parties and a few more miles the rebels were down on the ground pleading for the others to see reason. Getting back to the Civic was now secondary to exposing Rod as a maniacal liar. No matter how hard we tried and, despite the evidence of experience, we could not break the spell of the terrible twins. After traversing every street and back alley in Surry Hills twice over we finally ended up on Oxford Street. We were weary and frustrated but Rod and Chris were still going strong and still selling what they did not have. They led us down the road with all the girls giggling behind. Then, when we too tired too tired to carry on we stumbled across the perfect party at Fonzies. Fonzies was the first video game arcade in the city. It was half way down Oxford Street on the south side and was entered through a tunnel of neon tubes. It was the perfect place for the perfect party for tripping punks.

The tunnel of multi coloured flashing neon tubes got the acid boiling in our blood once more. The first thing that you saw when you entered was a full-sized horse on the far side of the room. Letting out a long, loud war cry Rod ran straight over to it and climbing on top he dropped a coin in the slot. It must be mentioned that Rod was sporting the second Mohawk haircut to be seen in Sydney. The first had been worn by Peer and how he had survived on the streets with it at thirteen is a story all on its own. Suffice it to say that while Rod was pretending to be an Indian Peer is pure Viking. Rod now stripped off his shirt to display his tattoos and loaded an imaginary bow with an imaginary arrow. He then took aim as we all dived for cover behind the machines and returned fire with our imaginary pistols. The other patrons stood staring with nervous smiles not sure whether to run or take cover themselves.

Rod sat imperiously upon his steed, impervious to our bullets. He then deliberately lined up each of the rebels one by one. He stared each of us directly in the eyes and then shot us through the heart. He was celebrating taking us for a ride by taking one himself and he had delivered the perfect party.

There were two adventures that revolved around the most iconic of Sydney symbols the Opera House. One when we were going out and one when we were going home. The Sydney Botanical gardens nestles snugly alongside the Opera House on the edge of the harbor. We would sometimes go there at night for punk picnics. It was like a little slice of punk paradise. On this particular occasion we were creeping through the trees like we were soldiers in the Vietnamese jungle. We were on a mission to reach the shore and escape by boat. Out of nowhere the skies were lit up with the radiation of rocket flares. It was so bright and the rockets fit so well into our fantasy that everyone stood stunned for several seconds. We were not sure whether we were under attack or just tripping so badly that we were imagining the whole thing. Finally, someone came to their senses and screamed. We all started running towards the Opera House gates in order to catch up with our sanity. The Botanical Gardens are locked at night so we had to scramble over the gates to escape our imaginary enemies. When we got to the Opera House forecourt, we were greeted by a classical orchestra playing Mozart. There was no one else anywhere to be seen. The fireworks that we had seen from the gardens went off again behind the orchestra. We were totally lost in our fantasy until someone called cut and we realized that they were filming an add.

The time that we were going home we had a terrifying encounter with the lone yobbo. We had been out for a night of destruction and debauchery and were trying to get home before the sun came up. Les had told everyone that if you were caught out tripping when the sun came up you were cursed to go on tripping forever.

We had decided to go back through the Botanical gardens. When we got to the forecourt of the Opera House, we found that it was filled punters slumbering in their sleeping bags. There must have been a huge event happening the following morning. We did not want to be delayed by disturbing them so we snuck through the bodies like we were making our way through a mine field. We were like punk pixies sprinkling our dust of delirium as we passed. We had almost made our way clear when one lone yobbo stood up. He was still about twenty meters behind us as he stretched his arms and yawned himself awake. When he saw us, he looked amazed but instead of being intimidated he started walking towards us. We were still obsessed by getting home before dawn so we walked away as quickly as we could without wanting to seem afraid. The yobbo obviously thought that we were afraid and was emboldened by our retreat. He came toward us without fear even though he was outnumbered by thirty to one. We led him on and started to pretend panic as we approached the gate. As he came nearer, we scrambled over the fence screaming in terror. When we were safely on the other side we waited and watched as the lone yobbo pressed himself against the gates and roared like a lion. We decided to picnic in the park and watch the sun coming up instead of going home to bed. We were less scared of security or of tripping forever than we were of the lone yobbo who we were sure would come and claim us in our sleep.

The punk population decided to take another trip. This path wound its way to some poor soul's house in Bathurst. Previous road trips had involved a handful of punks, this time we were a hundred more than a handful. We had been invited to perform at Bathurst College and several bands had decided to make the journey. Unlike the first trip to Canberra there were many more cars so we must have resembled a circus caravan as we careened down the road. There were also many more drugs by this time. While the early years of Punk had been fueled almost exclusively by alcohol a wide variety of stimulants were now employed. Some punks were hooked on downers so that they resembled Grandparents rather than Grandkids. Others preferred pot, speed or acid but at least heroine had not yet raised its ugly head. The vehicles were piled high with a mix of musical equipment and cartons of beer with the former becoming less important as the latter was steadily consumed.

Remarkably there was only one near fatal accident during the trip down as Charley raced his souped up six against Rob Millionaire's V8. We crested a hill like we were riding a roller coaster. No one even considered the consequences until Charley lost control. His car spun around several times without leaving the road. It was like we were driving on ice. If there had been any oncoming traffic, we would have been dead. When we finally came to rest, we were facing in the opposite direction and on the wrong side of the road. We sat in silent awe for several seconds before Pommy Ian declared 'that was great let's do it again!' Fortunately, Charley ignored his advice and we made it the rest of the way without further incident. We arrived like a marauding mess. There was no concern that we would be unable to entertain the students. Like all punk performances this trip was designed purely for our own pleasure.

It was a weekend and the University was deserted except for the few fools who had invited us. They now respectfully ushered us into the hallowed halls of learning. There was a lone security guard. He kept asking for our student cards and tried valiantly to keep us within whatever restricted area he deemed appropriate. This was like trying to talk a storm out of breaking. The gear was somehow setup and the bands did manage to play but the music was almost irrelevant to the fun being had. The ritual was performed and the spirit of total mayhem was summoned. The few wary students stared startled from the sidelines as we danced our way into oblivion. When we were finished, we were saved from the temptation to destroy public property by one of the students. This was just as well as otherwise the police would have undoubtedly been summoned and the party would have been over. The party was instead invited to move to the student's house for a destroy party. It seems as improbable now as it did then that anyone would consciously wish this kind of hell upon themselves. The student had obviously heard of the phenomena without ever experiencing it firsthand. The sense of celebrity that now surrounded certain members of the movement may have been motivation. It was like wishing that a tornado would attack your house so you could be on the news. Our response was incredulous but our reaction was automatic. We did not wish to disappoint our hosts and were eager to demonstrate just how flawed this idea really was. We piled back into our vehicles along with the aforementioned spirit of total mayhem and headed for the one place where we could really let it loose.

We arrived at the average looking suburban property fully fueled and really ready to rumble. We were so well organised for these occasions by this time that it took no time at all for marauding monster to find is feet. The techniques of destruction had been improved upon considerably over the years. People had now begun to specialize in various areas of demolition. Some small group of punks had developed a penchant for dismantling bathrooms and would know the most effective way of removing a bath and toilet by using parts of the shower. Others had identified household fixtures that could quickly be detached and used as tools for making holes in plaster walls. The various teams went quickly to work, proud of their professionalism and determined to destroy. It took some skill and experience to dislodge a bath and float it down the stairs. There was some quibbling over who would be involved and who would get to ride in the tub but this was all part of the process and only added fuel to the fire.

I remember standing in the kitchen watching the storm rage all around me. I was drunk and I was stoned and I was tripping. The tenant's nightmare was a beautiful dream to me. My dream was then interrupted when one of the Bathurst students approached me and asked if I remembered them. He was shaking my hand in a friendly but inappropriately formal manner. As I was having trouble seeing anything or anyone clearly by this stage, let alone remembering them, I shook my head. The strange student then began telling me a curious story in order to jog my memory. It turned out that we had been walking through Kings Cross one night when a police van had stopped and the cops had started arresting some hapless wino. My memory was returning and I began to try and focus more clearly on the face in front of me. When the strange student then said that we were locked up together and that his father was a lawyer my memory returned. My heart leaped and I felt sure that there was a God after all. The only decision I had to make was which of the three faces in front of me was the real one. I decided on the middle head as the safest option and swung hard. This was not a love tap. This was revenge that was served cold but suddenly got white hot. I did see this guy many years later at the Trade Union Club. He was so pleased to see me that he almost knocked me off my chair. He introduced me to his friends while bragging about how I had broken his nose. He demonstrated that being a victim of violence can sometimes be a good thing, depending on your point of view, life can be funny like that!

CHAPTER 13

The mass of mischief that was the Sydney Punk scene had moved its focus from Australia Street to a small block of one-roomed apartments on South Dowling Street. Just down the road from Fitzroy Street in Surry Hills. The building was a three-sided structure with the centre facing the street and two arms stretching back to form a courtyard. The place still stands and is now being used as a backpacker's hostel. At first, we shared the building with some arts school students from East Sydney Tech. Our over the top lifestyle soon became too much for them and they disappeared into the night. Annie had the large flat on one side of the building and Little Stewart had the same sized flat on the other side. An Asian girl with a crewcut named Lynne and an English girl with curly hair and an attitude named Fran had separate flats in the courtyard. I lived in the bottom floor flat on the left and Little Rob had the flat upstairs from me. Bailey and Pommy Ian lived on the right and other punks moved in and out or stayed there so often that it was hard to keep track.

Surry Hills had always been a working-class part of Sydney. For the first hundred years or so it was known as Irish Town. The streets had been filled with washing lines and rampant rats. A new kind of vermin had now come to infest the town in the form of yuppies. The contemporary contamination was like a plague to which there was no cure. Most of the streets around us were infected by the disease. The first sign of symptoms was pot plants appearing on the footpaths. This was a certain sign that the inhabitants of a property had caught the contagion. We could do nothing to stop the disease from spreading except keep ourselves safe. We tried to suppress the symptoms by stealing their supply of potted plants. But every time we returned in the evening they would be replaced and we were running out of room. We then began to return the original plants so the properties so that they became overwhelmed. Some with the sickness chained their pot plants to the wall to stop this circulation. This did not stop us from stealing them but meant that the pots were damaged when we returned them so they had to be disposed of by the owners. Sometimes there would be piles of broken pots placed outside of infected houses. It really became quite ridiculous. I'm sure that the yuppies thought that we were the vermin but we knew better!

We were in punk paradise and the party never stopped. I soon quit my job at the Housing Commission because I got tired of tripping over partied out punks in the courtyard on my way to work. I had recently transferred into head office in the old Anthony Hordern building in the city and had sat for six weeks shuffling the few bits of paper that could not be filed because they were incomplete. There was so little work the manager finally suggested that I start a training course to get out of the office. I told him that I wasn't going to be there that long. He told me that they had all said that when they were my age. I resigned on the spot because the prospect of doing no work at work was far worse than doing no work at home.

The flats were like an anarchist oasis in the midst of mindless mass consumerism. It was like a hippie commune without the countryside or the hippies. Many people have tried to establish a utopian ideal over the centuries. Thomas More's *Utopia* and Plato's *Republic* being the two most famous literary versions. The lack of individual ambition and the absence of money were two themes that were central to the success of the society in both cases. The punk scene had both of these qualities. The fluid nature of the social structure in the Sydney scene allowed individuals to find their own role and level. The small society established at South Dowling Street contained many strong individuals but their uniqueness only made sense and became apparent in the context of the overall movement. Punks like Rod Rodent, Chris Cross and Cathi Corpse were more central and essential to the scene than the bands that they went to see. The things people said and did socially provided a much simpler and more effective means of communication than what was said by singers in bands through the largely incoherent performance of lyric poetry. The uniform appearance stressed as essential to the success of a utopia was also present although individual style was also highly valued. The absence of money which was central to both literary utopias was fulfilled by circumstance as much as by choice. It also meant that scarce resources needed to be shared. If one person had money then everybody got drunk.

This was the pinnacle of punk culture. When once there had been no more than fifty hard core punks now there were hundreds. We would spend hours on weekends preparing for a night out. Everyone was wearing makeup and eyeliner was the most precious commodity in the community. The androgynous nature of the culture allowed everyone to share their clothes as well as their attitude. Some punks became hairdressers, some became makeup artists, others became amateur tattooists. Kiwi Kim began her career around this time and went on to run major tattoo parlours in Sydney in the years to come. Once the anarchist army was assembled, we would march from our mansion singing songs and cavorting our way through Surry Hills to the city. Since there was no other competing counter culture at the time and our dominance of the streets was unchallenged. The Generation X song 'One hundred punks rule' had now become a reality on the streets of Sydney. We also held sway over two major venues in the Civic hotel and Rags.

The problem with paradise and with any attempt to form any kind of utopia is that it is almost impossible to maintain in a pristine state. Plato pointed out that the world is in a constant state of flux. Once a state of perfection has been achieved degeneration must follow because change is inevitable. By helping to create a successful punk scene we had also ironically created a situation that was the antithesis of our own philosophy. We were suffering from the Frankenstein complex. We had created a monster that was beyond our control and which now threatened our very existence. We had chased the dream of a punk paradise and were now caught in the nightmare of a punk paradox. I began to believe that I needed to deconstruct my own image because punks that did not know me very well were starting to treat me like a star. How to achieve this without deconstructing my entire life presented an existential dilemma too great for me to come to grips with at the time. We had climbed the mountain and sat for a brief time at the summit but we all had to come down sometime.

The dissolution of the early punk scene was perhaps best demonstrated by the destruction of Rags. This was not achieved in a couple of hours as with a destroy party but over the last six months or so that we were in residence. Up until this time we had not destroyed our own venues and had shown respect to those who gave us sanctuary. The only things that suffered at the hands of punks at the Grand Hotel were the things that cost money. The jukebox was broken open and the contents replaced with punk singles. The pin ball machines were tampered with so that free games could be clicked up via the button at the back. The pool tables could be likewise lifted and dropped so that the balls would run out without the use of a coin. The slow and deliberate desecration of Rags demonstrated a totally different attitude. It reminded me of my mother saying that only a sick animal befouls its own nest. The toilets at Rags were the first organs of the body to display the symptoms of this disease. Pill heads and pissed off people who were generally new to the scene and trying hard to impress started to pull the doors off cubicles and smash the sinks and other fittings. This was not done as a celebration as it was with destroy parties but as a kind of slow, insidious suicide that reflected the personal problems of the perpetrators and did not reflect the original philosophical punk position.

I did go back to the flats at South Dowling Street years later. The punk population had moved on long ago. I had been out drinking with Animal and we had bumped into Bailey. He told us that most of the rooms were now vacant and that he had been put in charge. He said that we were welcome to stay if we wanted to. The place had deteriorated badly since we had left. It was like walking into a madhouse without the guards or padded cells. There was a mixture of androgynous ghouls and refugees from the streets with tear drop tattoos on their cheeks and monkeys on their backs. They roamed the corridors and entered rooms randomly. They were like resident spooks who were scared of themselves.

Bailey would walk through the halls swinging a large bunch of keys on a chain like a warder in an insane asylum. The same thing that he had done at the Police Station in Harris Street many years before. He would yell at the inmates and bang on doors as if he owned the place and the souls of all the insane. The inhabitants seemed more scared of him than whatever had scared them into this state in the first place.

I was given an upstairs room and tried to go to sleep but was woken up by one of the residents crawling along the roof of the verandah outside my window. This strange disheveled apparition stopped long enough to ask for a cigarette before continuing on to the next room once they knew that I had none. The fact that they were willing to risk life and limb by climbing around outside rather than risk meeting Bailey in the corridors sent a chill up my spine. The place had such an eerie feel that I could not settle and ended up walking all the way home to Newtown in the middle of the night. I was not afraid of Bailey but I was afraid of turning into one of the crazy ghouls that he had captured. The degeneration of the flats at South Dowling Street was a metaphor for the debilitation of the Sydney scene itself.

CHAPTER 14

After the renovation of Rags into a wreck the path of punk pandemonium led to the Heritage hotel in Kings Cross. Dave from Chaos married a barmaid from the Heritage Hotel and they are still together today. The Heritage was on a corner at the bottom of Kings Cross near the footbridge on Bayswater Road. It is now also a backpacker's hostel. It was a nice change from the Civic as the Heritage had a colonial style interior with wooden floors covered in plush carpet. The downstairs room had a bar that was square and protruded from one wall so that it divided the space neatly in two. The side where you entered had booths around the walls and tables in the centre. There was a pool table on the opposite side of the bar. The upstairs room had a bar on the right as you entered and toilets on the left at the end of the bar. You had to snake your way through a tight space between them in order to approach the stage. The stage was at the end of the room in front of a large window that showed the constant flow of traffic to and from the eastern suburbs. The floor upstairs was all bare wooden boards. The whole floor flexed when the place was packed and everyone was moving to the music.

The Heritage attracted a crowd that was not as hard core as the one at the Civic. It had been home to high-class whores and strippers from the Cross and many would still drop in for a drink. One of the weirdest was a girl named Jamie Jetson. She wore dayglo clothing with outrageous multi-coloured makeup and hair. She was as beautiful as she was mad. When she was arrested in London years later the papers said that she was the mirror of Marilyn Monroe. She was outrageous and vivacious and left men drooling in her wake. There was also a witch named Beth who had grown up in New Guinea as the daughter of a preacher man. She had large almond shaped, hazel eyes and very short black hair. She wore flowing black robes with a hood and looked like a wandering witch. Beth approached me at the pool table one night and asked me why I couldn't sink every ball on the table. She told me that my brain could instantly assess the angles and that it was only the distractions and doubts of my conscious mind that made me miss. I followed her advice and have trusted my first impressions ever since which has made me a much better pool player. I later named my second daughter after this most mysterious marvel.

Ed Kueper from the Saints would turn up to play at the Heritage in a band called the Laughing Clowns. The guitar player from Dragon also performed there looking like a lost soul. The Bedhogs were now in full swing and were popular with old and young punks alike. The Section also played their final gig at the Heritage Hotel. This was a shame but proved to be a bonus for us because Charley was now free to join our band. Rejex had been on holiday for some time. We had written a whole new set of songs as we had done the last time that we lost a drummer. We didn't even play the single because we felt that we had moved on as musicians. This alienated a lot of the young punks but we weren't performing to be popular. We believed that playing songs just to please punks was the same as selling out. This time around the music was much more accomplished. Richard and Nick were now using various effects boxes on their instruments that gave the sound a whole new feel. We were writing songs almost purely by jamming. This is still the best artistic feeling that I have ever experienced. Gigs are fine and encores are good but it is creation that provides the best buzz. When you are in a room with three other people and one starts to play a riff and everybody just joins in and the whole thing inspires a melody in your mind that you feel compelled to sing then nothing compares. It is a fluid process freed from ego as you give yourself selflessly to the song. The changes come naturally from the sub conscious rather than being orchestrated by careful consideration. The final product is like the punk movement itself. A collective expression of individual dreams and desires that can only be obtained by subsuming oneself to the collective consciousness.

We made our reappearance at the Heritage after doing our usual poster round of the entire city. Even though we felt that we had softened and some of our songs were quite slow the young punks didn't seem to notice. They pogoed with the same energy that had met Who wants to March or Eskyland. Danny Rumour was in the audience and said later that he had expected a miracle and almost got one. This was as close to a compliment as Danny was ever going to offer. He was the best musician in town and his judgements were always sincere and unerringly accurate. We were a great punk band but we were never going to achieve commercial success whether we wanted it or not. I remember Danny destroying the dreams of our old drummer Stuart after he debuted with his new Mod band The Sets. Stuart was looking quite weepy and said with sad eyes that Danny had told him that they were terrible. I told him that if Danny didn't like it, they may as well give up and they did shortly afterwards.

The Heritage Hotel was also of interest because it was the first place in which Space Invaders became available. I first experienced this new craze at a party at Charley's place at Clyde. This was the same house where we had auditioned him and where we had rehearsed the third and final version of Rejex. The usual suspects had arrived at the party early and we had dropped acid and smoked several bags of weed before the masses made their appearance. Scotch Jim arrived with his girlfriend Marie as if they were in fancy dress. He was dressed in a skin tight, silver jump suit that did nothing to hide his developing beer gut. Marie did her best to adopt a futuristic female form. He was very excited and insisted that I come with him up to the local hotel. I was reluctant to leave because the party had just started but he insisted that the expedition would change my life. This seemed hardly likely to happen at the local hotel in Clyde but I had to oblige him if only because it seemed so preposterous. When we entered the hotel, he took us to a small table which was one of several in the middle of the room. The table had a screen in the middle with little lights in funny shapes moving back and forth. We sat on either side and he put his twenty-cent coin in the slot and started playing. When my turn came, I applied myself as best I could and killed several armies before Jim demanded that I admit that I had played before. I told him that I hadn't but the game was just too easy on acid. I had destroyed his buzz and we returned to the party. We walked past Jimmy Bedhog threatening some young punk with a broken bottle and went to sit on the roof. We listened to the bands playing below while watching for some real aliens to appear in the skies above.

One of the strangest nights that I spent at the Heritage Hotel was when the Bedhogs were playing. Nick Sleaze and I had been at Kiwi Kim's place smoking some really good hash and had returned to the pub to see the rest of the set. The place was packed and the wooden floorboards were moving up and down like a trampoline. We squeezed our way past the bottleneck at the bar and stood on some stools at the side of the room. The band had just stopped for a break while someone changed a string and I noticed two guys move to stand against the wall near the stage. They were wearing blue jeans and cut off black T-shirts with black beanies and really wicked smiles. They stood with their arms folded and had looks on their faces like they wanted to lick their lips but didn't want to scare away their dinner. When the band started up again the young punks on the dance floor started slamming from side to side. The idea was to avoid being stuck on the end of the mass movement and being bashed into a wall.

Instead of being bashed into a wall the young punks were now being bashed by the two smiling strangers. The strangers stood with their backs against the wall and punched cleanly with both hands. It was like watching meat being fed into a sausage grinder. The young punks seemed unable to stop the dance. Despite the damage they continued to push each other into the punches. The carnage only came to an end when the song stopped. There was a pile of bodies in the middle of the dance floor and the two strangers still stood smiling maniacally with their backs against the wall. The young punks were busy helping each other to their feet. When the next song started the young punks started to dance as best they could. This time they bashed each other against one wall and then tried frantically to stop each other before got near the beanied boys. It would have been hilarious if it hadn't been so brutal. The two sadistic strangers soon got bored with watching this comic display and went downstairs for a drink.

When I went outside at the end of the gig the two strangers were jumping up and down on a car that belonged to the support band Local Product. The band were trapped inside and were screaming like they were in some cheap horror movie. This too was fairly funny and I wasn't sure whether my loyalty should be directed to the young punks or to the guys who were providing the entertainment. Jimmy Bedhog came out of the pub and stood next to me. I was beginning to fear that the punk scene that we had spent so many years putting together was about to be torn apart by the two boys in black. The car finally sped away and the two terrorists jumped off onto the road. They then turned their attention to us and walked towards us grinning. I don't mind admitting that I wasn't looking forward to the impending confrontation. To my surprise Jimmy started laughing and stepped forward to shake their hands. He then introduced me to his brother Tom and his best mate Hoggy. Tom had big brown eyes and short black hair and was as hard as he was humorous. Hoggy was tall and lean and just as mean. He had blue eyes, curly blonde hair and a handshake like a vice. They were Dilly boys from the Wollondilly Shire just south of Sydney. This was where the bushrangers had found sanctuary over a century ago. Looking at them you would have sworn that they were outlaws who had just come out of hiding from that 'impenetrable Bargo scrub.' They told me that they usually came into town to pick fights with bouncers because they found it hard to find a decent contest amongst the ordinary punters.

Fat Chris and I went rabbit hunting in Bargo the following weekend. The town of Bargo consisted of a pub, a railway station and a shop, at the time. Jim's family lived in a sprawling fibro house on four acres with a couple of horses and a dam. The block was adjacent to the roadhouse on the highway. Jim's mother Mike would walk across the paddocks to work at the roadhouse. Jim took me out to the small dam shortly after we arrived. He had a twenty-two rifle and shot a diver duck. The problem was that the dead duck was out in the middle of the dam. Jim decided to shoot the diver duck until it was moved to the edge of the dam. The duck was now full of lead and torn to pieces so it was inedible. Jim didn't care he was just happy that it was now a dead diver duck. We then went to Hoggy's house up on Razor back mountain and practiced shooting. Chris and I weren't much good but Hoggy hit everything. The Bargo boys got a good laugh watching us city slickers try to shoot. I thought it was hilarious that a guy named Hog lived on Razor back mountain.

That night we went out hunting. The main aim seemed to be annoying local landowners rather than the killing the local rabbits. The only thing that I can compare the evenings adventures to is the Australian movie classic 'Wake in Fright.' We were already drunk when the adventure began and drank as much as we could along the way. The only way to avoid being spotted by the land owners was to turn off the headlights and drive blind. This was how Jimmy went through the windscreen all those years ago. The Bargo boys knew the back roads so well that it did not concern them in the slightest. Hoggy tore down these dirt tracks at a top speed, twisting and turning to terrify the city boys in the back. The fact that it was impossible to see let alone spotlight any rabbits while driving this way escaped our attention at the time. At one-point a nearby house did light up and spotlights were pointed in our general direction. Shots were fired as we sped away causing the Bargo boys to hoot and holler in celebration.

Hoggy and Tom did manage to bag a few bunnies on the way back home. Chris fired a shot or two in anger but thankfully did not manage to hit us or anything else. As we turned up a track on the way home a hapless rabbit turned up in the middle of the road. Hoggy skidded to a halt while somehow still keeping the rabbit transfixed in his high beams. They handed me the gun and insisted that I bust my cherry. I got out of the car and tried to focus my bleary eyes on the target. I really couldn't miss from this range so I shut my eyes and pulled the trigger. The gun exploded in my hands and fell into pieces. I wasn't hurt but was so surprised that I stood stunned for a second. The rabbit was shocked from its trance and began trying to run up the bank at the side of the road. I had obviously hit it in the leg as it was having a hard time. Not sure what to do I ran after it intending to club it with the but end of the rifle. Hoggy jumped from the car and took it off me before I could wreck his gun. He then picked up the rabbit and snapped its neck like he was clicking his fingers. I guess that I was just not cut out to be a killer.

The only other thing that I remember about this weird weekend was the pub crawl the next night. The district and loyalties were divided between local townships. Each seemed to have a hotel and a football team. We started from the El Greco on the highway at Picton. This was neutral territory and had representatives from all the nearby tribes. They all sat sipping their schooners suspiciously screening for an impending scrap. It was as if trouble was inevitable and only a whisper away. We then went to the pub at Bargo where the boys were well known and equally well regarded. If there was going to be a fight at least it was going to be a fight amongst friends. We eventually ended up in enemy territory. I cannot remember the name of the pub but I do remember that there was a wire cage around the stage. We hesitated at the door long enough for Tom to whisper, 'alright so who are we gonna fight? I don't know whether it was Tom and Hoggy's reputations or just that the locals felt friendly that night but we did not get into a fight. The next thing I remember was waking up in my bed back in Bargo.

Meanwhile back at the Heritage Hotel Captain Chaotic invited a few of us outside to Colin Chaos' black Monaro for a session. The Captain then began to tell us a horror story that foretold the future of many of our friends. It was like we were children siting around a campfire except the only light was from lighters lighting the bong. Captain Chaotic and Colin worked on the railways. A lot of punks worked on the railways at the time but no one really worked there. There was one punk who worked two jobs. He had a railway carriage set up for sleeping during the day so he was fresh for his real job at night. The Captain told us that some guys at the railways had asked him if he could score some smack. He had asked them if they had used before. They had assured him that they had. He had warned them that the gear he would score would be pure so they had better be used to it. After being certain that they were sincere the captain procured the heroine. They all met up in a storage shed in the railway yards to do the deed. There were seven people in the shed. The Captain mixed up and personally shot them all up before fixing himself. The Captain paused at this point in his story and stared at us over the front seat to make sure that he had our full attention. He then told us in his gnarly, high pitched voice that everyone in the shed had overdosed. It was fortunate that someone else had wandered in looking for a place to take a nap otherwise, the Captain said, everyone in the shed would be dead!

CHAPTER 15

Little Stewart had moved into a flat with Pommy Ian and others in Woomera Avenue just across the walkway from the Heritage Hotel. Stewart had a Fender twin reverb with wheels that he would ride across the footbridge when the Bedhogs were playing. The house became home to The Smoker's Club. This was an association of punk veterans from the Western Suburbs who liked to smoke pot. It was an elite organisation as the punk scene had grown much too big for us to include everybody. Every Friday night we would gather at the flat with as much pot as we could muster or an equivalent amount of money. Neither was a prerequisite for attendance. Paul who did not have a car and Pommy Ian would sit in the centre of the room and roll the largest joints possible. The rest of us would sit around the room in anxious anticipation. When the rolling was completed each person would be given a massive joint. We would then all light up at the same time and pass the joints around to the left until the entire stash was consumed. Pommy Ian would then call for a rope because we felt like we were about to float away.

This might seem like just another session and a scene that could have been repeated anywhere in Sydney at the time but it was more than this. This was a ritual to celebrate the fact that those present had been present at the original punk rock ritual at the Grand Hotel. It was the recognition that the people present had been instrumental in establishing the punk rock scene in Sydney and had survived long enough to enjoy the fruits of our labour. It may have been silly and conceited but it was also well deserved. When the smoking was finished, we would sit for several moments in silence and look around the room through the haze, waiting for the smoke to dissipate and for someone to break down in inevitable laughter. When the laughter was over, we would rise as one and gather our coats before floating across the bridge to whatever was awaiting us at the Heritage Hotel that night.

Not all of our adventures happened at night. On sunny Saturday afternoons we would gather in the downstairs bar of the Heritage to listen to the blues stylings of Gypsy Dave Smith. On sunny Sundays we would go on pub crawls on and around William street sipping Coopers Sparkling Ale. Little Stewart had become a wine connoisseur and got a good laugh when he once declared that 'wines weren't wines.' He had also become a reggae junky and would talk about reggae legends as if they were long lost friends. Nick Sleaze and I had started listening to classical music and would debate whether Beethoven or Mozart was superior although we both loved Bach. Nick would insist that Beethoven was better but I said that Beethoven was just heavy metal Mozart. There were many trips up the road to Kings Cross during the week. We would go to the Jazz Club every Wednesday night. It was downstairs in what had been just another strip joint. Students from the Conservatorium of Music would go there to let off steam after their studies. We would sit and sip wine from the cheap carafes and silence anyone that dared to talk while the musicians were jamming. We were enjoying a genteel retirement after we had won the war. We felt that we had nothing left to prove and could now relax and indulge in whatever life had to offer with an abundance of self-satisfaction.

The Heritage had become like a retirement home for old punks. Young punks rarely visited the Heritage and still inhabited the

Civic Hotel on weekends. The major difference between the two scenes was that the sense of individual style that had marked the early era of the Punk scene in Sydney had been washed away by a sea of black. The young punks displayed a disappointing uniformity. They all wore black jeans and black leather jackets. The colourful sense of celebration that had marked the early scene seemed to have been replaced with a funereal feel. I countered this new culture by trying to appear as sharp and as clean as possible. I cut my hair very short and dyed it very blonde. I wore a body shirt with green and black vertical stripes under a heavy navy jacket with big brass buttons. I still wore skintight black stovepipes and shiny black boots so my appearance was still punk but was distinctive enough for me to mistaken as a trendy. The scene was now so big that not everyone knew each other. This meant that it was now possible for the golden rule to be broken and punks could now end up fighting punks.

This problem became apparent at the Heritage Hotel one night when my punk past came back to haunt me. I was walking up the stairs with an effete friend when a young punk kicked a can that almost me in the head. I told the punk to pull his head in as we went up to the band room and gave the matter little further thought. We were busy watching the band when the young punk returned and tapped me on the shoulder. He was accompanied by one of the first people that I ever saw in Sydney who was dressed as a skinhead. The young punk then asked me outside while the skinhead stood staring at me with his best scary face. I was unsure whether I should introduce myself in order to avoid the confrontation or embrace my anonymity and let the cards fall where they may. I decided on the latter course because I was still trying to deconstruct my star like status.

It was a strange sensation being treated like a trendy by a young punk who had no idea who I was. When I got outside there was a large group of young punks sprawled around the pavement looking like they were homeless alcoholics. I saw Animal amongst them and he smiled at me as I walked passed. I went straight passed him and a little way up the road to take off my jacket and throw it a doorway. This drew catcalls from the crowd who assumed that I was walking away. They soon shut up when I turned around and walked back to face my antagonist. The young punk was playing to the crowd and decided to mimic me by taking off his own jacket in a mocking, theatrical manner. I couldn't believe my luck and almost laughed as I hit him under the chin with a hard-right hand. His arms were still pinned to his sides by his coat so I continued to punch him down the road. He twitched around like he was being electrocuted inside a straight jacket. He then started pleading with me to let him take off the coat. This just made the whole situation even more comical. He eventually fell down bleeding in the gutter. I went to retrieve my coat from the doorway. As I walked back past him into the pub he started yelling that he was going to get me later. I told him that he would have to wait until he grew up. This was a reference to him being a young punk and even though I was an old punk I was probably still younger than the guy in the gutter.

As I sat drinking in the downstairs bar news of the fight had begun to circulate. Animal came in to congratulate me. He told me that the young punk had a knife and was planning to stab me when I left the pub. I wasn't sure what to do but about this but decided not to let it ruin my night. I went back upstairs to see the end of whatever band was playing. At the end of the gig I walked down the stairs and saw the young punk coming up. I decided to confront him inside where we were surrounded by people. The congestion on the stairs would make it harder for him to use his knife or for his friends to back him up. I got to him before he could see me and grabbed him by the jacket. I pushed him hard up against the wall and asked him straight out if he really intended to stab me. To my surprise he became instantly apologetic and asked me if I was really Johnny Rejex. When I told him that I was he put out his hand for me to shake. He said that his name was Andrew and that he was a friend of Trog from Canberra. He told me that he had always wanted to meet me. I burst out laughing and we went out drinking afterwards.

This most outrageous escapade around the time of the Heritage Hotel happened one night at a party at the Particles place. It was in Bourke Street and was just down the road from Darlinghurst Police Station. The Particles were art school students from East Sydney Tech who represented the only other version of youth culture around the streets of Sydney at the time. They were like distant cousins to the punks. They dressed in order to display their difference from main stream society but not extreme enough to appear as a threat. The two cultures would sometimes contact but never really connected. Art school types were generally isolated individuals dreaming of future recognition while we were all about the collective and dreaming of no future at all. This particular particle party was quite quiet and people were politely cracking open wine bottles and beer cans or cracking on to each other or cracking jokes. The party goers included the Kiwi connection. Guys like Hoody who went on to help form the Allniters and the Johnnys and Jamrag who played in a band called Proud Scum. There were also a couple of Kiwi girls named Sue and somebody who had opened a clothes shop in Oxford Street. The mood was mild and bordering on pretentious. It was the very mood that usually invited punk displays of destruction but everyone was feeling friendly. Thoughts of madness and mayhem were the farthest things from our minds. The peace of the party was only interrupted when Peter Particle came into the kitchen and carefully circulated the room reminding all the punks present that 'this was not a destroy party.'

It might not be the stupidest thing a person could say in such circumstances but I really struggle to think of something stupider.

No one had even considered the idea of a destroy party until it was mentioned by this particular Particle. The chant soon went up around the room and then around the entire party as punks began informing each other that 'this was not a destroy party.' Plates and glasses were soon being smashed to accompany this chant. The hapless Particle panicked and became more excited in his remonstrations. The accompanying sounds of destruction escalated in response. 'This is not a destroy party' people would say as they overturned the fridge. 'This is not a destroy party,' someone else would yell as they threw something through a window. Pretty soon the whole party and the Particle's entire world had descended into utter chaos.

It had been a long time since we had had a destroy party. It took a while for people to remember their roles. At least we remembered to turn off the gas before tearing the stove off the wall and throwing it through the window. Pretty soon the demolition was in full swing. But even all our experience and expertise were not enough on this occasion to dismantle the stairs. Terry the doorman had to go home to his squat in Woolloomooloo to get a sledge hammer and a couple of crowbars to do the job properly. The Particle's house also had a balcony outside the top floor bedroom that hung out over the footpath on Bourke Street. A number of us decided to jump up and down on it until it was dislodged into the street. The most remarkable thing about this act was not that it was so dangerous but that the Police Station was within full view the whole time and no one there seemed to notice. It was probably the most damage caused by punks in one instance until Mick Lips hunted down Dick Smith's helicopter with a two by four some years later. Terry told me later that after they had removed the stairs a punk had walked over the edge of the top floor while eating a large jar of mayonnaise. The jar had shattered against his chest when he hit the floor. When Terry took him to be treated at St Vincents Hospital the staff were reluctant to touch him because they thought he had been the victim of some bizarre sexual assault. When Terry tasted the offending substance in order to prove them wrong the staff screamed and ran away in disgust.

After the party we were walking up Bourke Street towards Taylor Square when one of the neighbors came out onto his front porch to abuse us. He was wearing shorts and a dirty singlet and seemed more than a little bit drunk. He had a bat in his hand and two small terriers barking around his feet. Jimmy decided to attack him and ran into the yard. He tackled the guy to the ground and started yelling at us to join in but no one moved a muscle. It was not in our nature to attack innocent civilians. Ganging up on some drunk guy for protecting his property was not part of our purview. Jimmy and the homeowner wrestled around the front yard with Jimmy still yelling out for help. The two terriers decided to get involved and started biting Jimmy on the buttocks. The whole thing became so funny that punks were falling over on the footpath laughing. Jimmy finally extricated himself from the guy and his dogs and ran out of the yard. He railed and ranted at us for not helping him but no one bothered to reply because the whole thing was just too funny for words.

It was also when we were hanging out at the Heritage that we started playing sport. This was highly unusual for punks but as the sporting contests themselves provided a kind of parody they still suited our style. The games were held in the leafy up market suburb of Rose Bay against a backdrop of the yachts in Rushcutters Bay Park. The games started with a few friends on weekends and eventually attracted most of the punk population. There would be fifty or sixty punks out on the oval playing soccer or rugby league and as many on the sidelines watching. It was like a picnic day for punks. The perversity of the situation was not lost on the Rose Bay residents who would stop walking their dogs long enough to stare with their mouths agape before hastily moving on to the safety of their homes.

My favourite game was played in the mud and pouring rain. Charley and I organised all the Westies to play what was left of the North Shore punks. Charley was a former halfback who liked to tackle low and hard. I was a former lock forward and loved using my shoulders on bigger guys. Together so we made a great tackling team. We smashed a big guy named Tristan so hard that he could hardly walk. We ended up injuring so many of the opposition that the game had to be called off through sheer lack of numbers. No one cared about the score because it was not a matter of winning or losing. It was a matter of putting on a spectacle and reminding the middle-class members of society that there was a threat in their faces. The games were played in full punk gear so that belt buckles and badges often caused more cuts and bruises than the tackles. It was the absurdity of the entire event that made the games worthwhile but we were just teenage kids after all. It was weird that being so violent reminded us of our innocence, life can be funny like that!

CHAPTER 16

After the disintegration and desecration of the flats in South Dowling Street I was invited to share a house with Fenton and his girlfriend Dorothy. They had a small terrace house in a small alleyway behind Oxford Street. It was the first time that I had lived in a fairly settled domestic situation since leaving home. Fenton and Dorothy both worked and lived like a married couple. There was always food in the fridge and even toilet paper instead of newspaper in the bathroom. At night I would go for long walks down Oxford Street through Hyde Park and down into the Domain. I could then sit on the foreshores of the harbor to watch the water and wonder about the world. The city was a very peaceful place late at night and the fact that you could still stroll through parkland for a couple of kilometers without meeting anyone saved my sanity several times.

On other nights Pommy Ian and I would sit up all night taking drugs and watching television. Sometimes we would go and sit on Gilligan's Island eating hamburgers from the Four Seasons while we watched the world pass by. It was not long before Dorothy began to resent our freedom and the fact that she had to step over our prostrate bodies early each morning on her way to work. Dorothy had become famous when Les had talked her into looking for gas leak with a lit match in the oven at Australia Street. She lost every single hair on her head in the ensuing explosion.

She looked like an alien for ages because she had no eyebrows. I saw her face on a political poster many years later as a candidate for the Lord Mayor of Sydney. I thought that this was pretty funny considering her punk past and her dubious public safety record. She was too much of a politician to be a punk and too much of a punk to be a politician.

I was soon saved from this domestic bliss when Jimmy moved out of a house in Fitzroy Street and I moved in. The house in Fitzroy Street was built as the city residence of a wealthy country gentleman. You entered through a hallway that had a large room to the right that had double doors opening onto the lounge room. The lounge room led out to a rather large kitchen that seemed more appropriate for a small hotel. The stairs at the end of the hall led up to the master bedroom. There was a small room for a study attached at the landing. Towards the back of the house there was another small room that must have been a dressing chamber or walk in wardrobe. You had to go through it in order to get to the bathroom. The master bedroom was right at the top of the stairs at the front of the house and had a closed in verandah. This was the only real bedroom in the house but this did not prevent us from filling the place with punks.

We had various people at various times throughout these rooms. Fat Chris and Bailey and Robin, who was not Slim Jim's sister, all lived there at different times. There was also a guy named Gerard who was studying to be a lawyer. He had decided to be a drug dealer in the meantime. The problem was that Rob Millionaire lived just two doors up the road and was already a well-established and very reliable dealer. Gerard always had drugs but never bothered to blow us out. This was a bitter bone of contention that soon became a deal breaker. We decided to raid his stash one day when we were bored. We discovered his supply of Buddha sticks not very well concealed in a coat pocket. I just wanted to take a couple but Fat Chris decided that he wanted to make a statement.

He took a pair of scissors and cut the sticks in half before putting the broken remains back in the pocket. Gerard came home and raced upstairs as usual without even saying hello. He soon let out a scream that would have woken the dead. He never said a word about what had happened because he realised that he could do absolutely nothing about it. He moved out soon afterward.

Fat Chris and Bailey never really got on and almost came to blows on several occasions. I had to admire Bailey's courage. He didn't stand a chance in a fistfight with Chris but he never backed down. The constant aggravation soon took its toll and Bailey surrendered his place in the house rather than surrender his pride or blood. Robin was the next to leave. This was not because of any personal antagonism but because she kept bringing home young punks like stray animals. Some of these strays were from Local Product and other new punk bands. Robin would bounce into the lounge room bubbling with anticipation. Her new punk partner would wait in the hall as if we were Robin's parents and they were afraid to face us. Robin would smoke a couple of cones while Chris growled and punched things to scare her prospective partners. When she had finally had her fill, she would bound up the stairs with the young punk following behind her like a grateful puppy. She soon moved out because her punk parents couldn't put up with these pathetic puppies.

We told each of the people that moved out that they still had to continue paying rent until we got some punk to replace them. We never looked for anyone else and only Bailey failed to comply. Jimmy's little sister Bin soon moved in to take his place. We now had a palatial residence with only three residents. We now had enough space to stretch out and enjoy ourselves like landed country gentry. I was in the front room which also served as a rehearsal space for the band. There were very few rehearsal studios at this time. The only one that was always operating and was always cheap was Studio Twenty. It was on Bourke Street just around the corner from Taylor Square. The studio consisted of a small padded room that was always hotter than hell. It was nestled amidst a pile of wreckage that mainly comprised of second-hand speakers and old amps. There was also any number of unnamed miscellaneous mechanical devices that someone had spent years collecting but no time at all considering.

We left the musical gear set up in my bedroom. My little brother would have great fun playing with Charley's drum kit when he came to stay. In order to entertain him I would occasionally pull a prank. Once when Fat Chris and I were tripping I told Joe to go into the lounge room and keep an eye on Chris who was watching the television. Joe sat in the opposite arm chair as I went out into the backyard to get the shovel. I then came screaming into the room and aimed the shovel at a point on the wall just over Chris' head. The shovel hit the wall with a clang that removed a large hunk of plaster. Chris almost had a heart attack. He wasn't sure whether to kill me or join in our laughter but it was all in the name of good clean fun.

We were about to have even more fun when we heard that the Stage Door Tavern was closing down. No punk bands had ever played at the Stage Door but we had gone there on Wednesday nights because it was free. The only reason that we were aware of the place closing down was because it was advertised on a television news show. The fact that the place was closing was of less interest to us than the reporter saying that there was going to be a riot. This news spread like wildfire amongst the punk community. We soon had several people knocking at our door outraged by the report. If there was going to be a riot in Sydney then we believed that we should have been consulted. The announcement was obviously part of some publicity stunt arranged by management. It certainly wasn't part of the culture of Midnight Oil who were playing the gig. It could also have been a ploy by the police propaganda unit in order to preempt any trouble. We were insulted and suspicious and totally uncertain about what we should do. We could not stop the riot because this would have meant going against everything that we didn't believe in. We could not support the riot because this meant supporting the publicity stunt and supporting a band that we wanted nothing to do with because of their political posturing.

We were still ambivalent about our response on the night that the Stage Door Tavern closed. Several people thought that we would only encourage them by attending. Several others had the smell of a riot in their nostrils and were proving difficult to restrain. We eventually decided that doing something was better than doing nothing. A group of us walked down to the site to see what was happening mainly because there was nothing happening anywhere else. We were very cautious in our approach, like dingoes circling a snare. The advertising campaign still seemed like some sort of trap. It had aroused our survival instincts much more as our curiosity. We eventually approached through Belmore Park which was opposite the venue and provided some sort of cover from the police who were everywhere.

The Stage Door Tavern was located in the basement floor of a business building that was the only building on the block. The rest of the space around the building was a car park surrounded by cyclone fencing. The cops had surrounded this entire area and were almost close enough together to be holding hands. This seemed like a gross overreaction. The threat was only implied by the media and the crowd was mainly made up of surfies from the southern suburbs. These people had no interest in the survival of an inner-city music venue so the whole situation still smelled strange. We circled the block several times and eventually felt assured enough to go down the stairs that lead to the venue. The set was coming to a close and the vibe seemed fairly positive so the mystery of the advertised riot remained unresolved. Despite the lack of any evidence of impending trouble we did not feel safe at the front doors as there was nowhere to go if something did start and the police got nasty. We eventually went back over to the park and sat on a bench waiting for the mystery to resolve itself.

The mystery was compounded instead when a big blue bus arrived. It stopped outside the top of the stairs and a whole bunch of police dressed like spacemen jumped out. They then marched with military precision and made two lines adjacent to the exit like they were forming a guard of honour. They wore blue uniforms with black boots and black motorcycle helmets. They also carried big Plexiglas shields and looked like they were Storm Troopers from a Star Wars movie. This was the first time that the new riot police had been deployed and they provided a superb spectacle. The fact that they were riot police meant that there had to be a riot so we settled in to enjoy the show.

As the gig came to a close people started leaving the venue and filing through the two lines of hard-core cops. They exhibited curiosity rather than animosity and began to gather around our spot on the bench. They would have gone straight across the park to Central Station if they hadn't been so intrigued by the alien police presence. One guy did approach the police lines and went up to each cop individually in order to stare them in the eyes from close range. The coppers didn't flinch but stood like Grenadier guards seemingly impervious to his presence. Once the lone terrorist had got past the police he spun around and dropped to one knee. He then began pretending to spray them with machine gun fire. The crowd cheered him on and the police began to bristle. We realised that the fantasy fight was soon going to become very real and was not going to be funny at all. We went over to the side of the park near the railway line and climbed up on sandstone toilet block. Our position provided a perfect perspective and also meant that we were relatively safe from the police when whatever trouble they were planning started.

In hindsight the appearance of the riot police at this time had nothing to do with the closing of the Stage Door Tavern. The N.S.W. Police force had recently suffered several humiliating experiences at the hands of bikers at the Bathurst races. On the last occasion the Police had decided to build a cage out of cyclone fencing to one side of the racetrack. This was meant to be a temporary prison for members of the crowd who got too drunk or delinquent. The problem was that the police were outnumbered the bikers by at least one hundred to one. The crowd were also more than a physical match for the cops. They did not like the idea of being imprisoned on open display on what was essentially their big day out. After a few boisterous bikers had been locked up the rest of the crowd decided to free them. The police were overwhelmed and became so flustered that they ended up taking refuge in the very prison that they had erected to contain the crowd. The imprisoned police were then pelted with beer cans and bottles filled with urine until reinforcements arrived. The fact that no police were killed or seriously injured was testament to the tolerance of the crowd rather than the proficiency of the police.

We were now witnessing the over reaction to this recent humiliation. As the crowd in Belmore Park increased in size and restlessness the danger to them increased as well. The police were obviously there to test their boots and batons even though there was no real threat of a riot breaking out. As the standoff continued some hoodlums at the back of the crowd started throwing bottles and cans at the police lines. This drew mild applause from the crowd but did little or no damage to the police. The crowd did not expect anything to happen and were mocking the impotence of the police rather than trying to initiate anything. We were growing weary of the wait but we were still wary. Some punks wanted to leave but we did not want to give up our excellent view of the expected excitement. We decided that our refuge on the roof was still the safest spot. We knew that we were the most likely people to be arrested even if we were not involved in the coming conflict. We were just discussing our exit strategy when Pommy Ian began making a speech to the crowd that was reminiscent of Shakespeare's Henry V. It culminated with him standing at the end of the toilet block with one arm dramatically raised in the air as he screamed 'charge!' As if in response to his clarion call the police charged across the road and into the crowd with batons raised and shields at the ready.

We watched from above as the police set about brutally bashing male and female patrons alike. They drove the crowd of kids like cattle across the park towards Central Station. We cheered on the police and pointed out several people who were trying to escape. There was no riot and not even any resistance. It was a brutal and one-sided display of state sanctioned violence. We stayed long enough for the police line to pass us by before climbing down and racing around the corner to the relative safety of the streets of lower Darlinghurst. Some punks stayed to enjoy the ensuing pandemonium. Bailey was arrested for jumping up and down on the rooves of several police cars. He was later acquitted when he threatened to sue for police brutality. Bailey had the Devil's own luck but the police obviously didn't want an investigation into the incident. We went home feeling that our suspicions had been justified. Happy that the mystery of the advertised riot had been resolved. We were still not happy that a riot had been planned without our permission but felt that the event was well worth witnessing anyway. The fact that the riot police had caused a riot made perfect sense to us at the time because the behaviour of all N.S.W police squads logically proceeded from their official titles. The Drug Squad dealt drugs, The Vice Squad ran prostitution, the Gaming Squad ran the illegal casinos and members of the Armed Hold Up Squad had recently been arrested for committing armed hold ups in Melbourne. So, it was no real surprise the Riot Squad had started a riot.

CHAPTER 17

The Civic continued to be the central hub of the scene for several years. It was mainly a recruitment station for young punks and a venue for new punk bands. Legends like Les Wreckage would still wander in occasionally to supervise the scene. I stayed away because I did not like the way that the young punks spoke to you in wide eyed wonder because you were in a band. The alternative was that they were sizing you up to take you down in order to enhance their status. One night when I was there a group of old punks were standing around outside reminiscing when we wondered whether we were in a time warp. A group of young people were standing on the opposite corner showing off their sixties fashion sense. One of them turned to us and said, 'punk's dead it's the nineteen eighties!' Chris Cross shot back with 'yeah, so why are you dressed like it's the nineteen sixties?' She had no response to that and stormed off, followed by her friends and our deserved derision. We all had a laugh about it but did not realise at the time that these people were serious. They considered themselves to be a part of a brand-new youth culture. This was despite the fact that they were wearing what was a recycled fashion that had been fairly ordinary the first time around. Not only was the fashion recycled but punks who had failed to make an impression on the scene had also started to recycle themselves as mods. As Peter Wells said years later 'it might have made sense if they had called themselves post mod" but they didn't so it made no sense at all.

The first recycled punks that I saw were Kevin and Gerard who had already changed from punks to communists and were now standing outside a party in Woomera Avenue dressed up as rude boys. They were surrounded by a group of young punks who were determined to do them harm. I had to intervene because Kevin and Gerard had been my friends but also because they had been punks long before their assailants had fastened on their first safety pins. The young punks argued that if the mods did not want to be attacked then they should not go around with targets on their backs. I thought that this was fair enough and we had a good laugh about it. While we were laughing Kevin and Gerard took off down the road. Fortunately for them the young punks did not think that they were worth chasing.

Mods soon started to spring up like mushrooms. It was a safe and clean way for suburban kids from affluent backgrounds to access the inner-city scene without worrying their parents. There didn't seem to be a scene as there were no mod bands or mod houses. There was just a bunch of effete fashion victims riding into the city on the weekend on scooters. The fact that they could afford scooters at all demonstrated how truly middle class the whole thing was and just how sad the Sydney scene was becoming. They all began to gather at the Sussex Hotel on the edge of the city. It was similar to the Civic Hotel in style but smaller and smellier. We had played there a couple of times but were eventually banned because Rod Rodent threw a glass at the stage hoping to hit Don Ego. Rod always denied that he did it which made us certain that it was him. Rod later dressed as a rude boy and played bass in a band called the Singles with Andrew from the Broken Toys. He even began calling himself Rod the Mod in an average attempt to attract a new crowd and ride what turned out to be a very insignificant wave.

The first confrontation we had with the Mods was when Jimmy Bedhog took offence to something that was said by an ex-young punk called Bill Posters. He was a nerdy looking kid who obviously hadn't heard of Rocks. No one was really interested in Jimmy's vendetta but we were bored on a Saturday afternoon at Fitzroy Street and Jimmy's enthusiasm could be contagious. Jimmy, Fat Chris, Little Rob and I all piled into Rob Millionaire's V8 and headed into town. We parked just around the corner from the Sussex Hotel and walked to the pub. We didn't have a plan but no one ever knew what Jimmy was going to do so we just followed him in. Bill Posters was sitting at the bar with his stringy thinning hair and thick glasses. Although the pub was full of his fellow mods Jimmy walked right up to him, removed Bills' glasses, and punched him right in the nose. He then put his glasses back on which made Bill look rather comical, wobbling on his stool with watering eyes and askew spectacles. We were taken by surprise as there was usually some sort of verbal exchange before punches were thrown in these situations. There would have been thirty or forty Mods in the bar at the time. This meant that we were outnumbered by about ten to one. We stood for several seconds like gunslingers waiting for the other guy to make the first move. Jimmy then turned and walked out of the bar as if nothing had happened. We followed him out onto the street looking over our shoulders. We were certain that some of the mods would want to defend their friend but not one mod moved a muscle.

We stood on the footpath and waited several seconds before bursting into laughter. We couldn't believe Jimmy's nerve or the lack of response. It took a little while for the adrenaline to settle and our relief to turn to disappointment. We were all worked up and ready to rumble. Fat Chris then decided to demonstrate his disappointment. The mods scooters were parked outside the pub. He kicked the first one so hard that it caused a chain reaction and they tumbled down the hill like dominos. We braced ourselves for battle again, certain that the mods would be forced to defend their property even if they wouldn't defend their friend. After waiting for several more seconds on high alert we gave up and went back to the car. I started to tell this story recently to a guy that I worked with because he said that he and been a mod. He interrupted me by saying that he knew the story well and that it had become a part of Mod folklore. The fact that mods would retell a story of their own humiliation is almost more embarrassing than the scene itself.

The mods did try to take their revenge by paying some skinheads to attack us at Side FX. Side FX was a disused school at the back of Kings Cross. The school operated as a day care centre and was run by the mother of punk sisters Monique and Michelle. It had a large hall that opened onto the street and a stage that was perfect for bands. One night when Rejex were playing the venue was assaulted by skinheads. Skinheads had arrived on the scene at the same time as mods. I still don't understand what the skinheads were all about. They were like sharpies without the cultural context. Skinheads in England were all about soccer clubs and local turf but the skinheads in Sydney had none of these things. Many of them had cockney accents but had never been to the East End of London. They were the kind of kids who liked to torture their pets and other small animals and were like the mod's meaner bother boy brothers. The odds started out even but the mods ran away as soon as the rumble started. The skinheads tried their best to test our metal but they never got through the doors. Some young punk ran up to the stage to tell me what was happening but I didn't believe them. There is a photo of me on stage smiling at the camera while making a peace sign. The skinheads had stormed the barricades but were beaten back by the Blacktown boys and Terry who was in fine form.

After the fight Terry told me that Jimmy had been fighting next to him on the steps, kicking skinheads back into the streets. During a brief pause in the proceedings Jimmy had turned and punched

Terry right in the throat. When he asked Jimmy why he had done it Jimmy had said that he thought that he would never get a better chance to take down the legend. Terry was too flabbergasted to take his revenge or do anything other than recover. Jimmy's personality was a constant conflict between contradictions.

One night at Woomera avenue I had asked him why he beaten a couple of young punks at the Civic. The young punks hadn't really done anything and it seemed like Jimmy was just being a bully. He told me that it because of his cancer. He said that sometimes he just got angry and needed to hit something. He seemed sincere and I offered to be his punching bag. I suggested that the next time he felt that way he should come and see me and we would go over the park and fight. That way no innocent people needed to suffer as it would just be a fight amongst friends. Jimmy changed from weeping victim to a vicious victimizer instantly. He suggested that we do it right now. I was taken aback and unsure whether he was serious. He persisted and I reluctantly agreed so we went outside. We faced off in the street with all of the other household members standing around in eager anticipation. I really didn't want to do it and waited for him to make the first move. When nothing happened, I decided to push him rather than punch him. Jimmy fell backwards onto the footpath and lay there smiling. He kept saying things like 'see it doesn't matter' and 'it's all bullshit' like he was some kind of guru. I was so baffled that I gave him a hand to get up and we went back inside to get drunk. I never thought that he was afraid of a fight and never believed that he had just backed down. It was bizarre and bewildering behavior which was precisely what Jimmy was.

On another night we had been outside Arthurs' nightclub in Kings Cross. It was a very trendy hangout for rich kids with kinky connections. Jimmy and I were sitting on a wall watching people going in and out when we saw some young trendy dressed as a punk. Jimmy couldn't resist and ran over to tear the guys already torn t-shirt right off his back. The guy ran into the club screaming while Jimmy and I sat back on the wall laughing with him waving the t-shirt in the air like a victory pennant. The next thing the doors of the club flew open and a dozen trendies ran out led by the bouncer. We took off up Victoria Street with the posse of posers right on our heels. I have always been as slow as a wet week so the bouncer soon caught up. I knew this because he hit me on the head with an iron bar. The first time was just a tap and he was obviously showing off for his friends. The second time he hit me a bit harder and I knew that the third time would knock me out. I stopped and turned around yelling at Jimmy to do the same. The posse stopped and the bouncer stepped forward and kicked me under the ribs. It hurt like hell but he was still just playing to put on a show. The second time he kicked me I noticed that he jumped onto his left foot first. The next time he stepped onto his left foot I stepped into him and threw off his timing and balance. I threw a left jab that caught him right under the chin. He paid the price for playing around and ended up flat on his back and out cold. The posse panicked at the fall of their hero and ran back down the road to the club. I turned around to see that Jimmy had run up the road and was now waiting for me up on the corner. Jimmy was responsible for many devious and dastardly deeds but they never seemed to damage his reputation. It was like he was surrounded by a force shield that somehow sheltered him from any negative nuance and only let the good get in.

Jimmy was also responsible for discovering another great venue that we helped to establish. Jimmy and Little Rob came over to Fitzroy Street one afternoon to tell us a great new club that they had found while wandering around. We got dressed up that night and went down to Foveaux Street on the way to Central Station in order to check out the new turf. The Trade Union Club was three floors high with ample floor space but there was virtually no one there. We wandered through the downstairs bar and hardly raised a whisper because the few geriatrics in attendance were so focused on the poker machines. They would probably not have noticed if the whole place burned down. The downstairs bar smelled of stale beer and cigarettes and the fetid flesh of the soon to be departed. Jimmy and Rob then saved us from this purgatory by taking us up to the next level which was like paradise in comparison. The whole floor was filled with full sized snooker tables that no one was playing. There was a bar to the left but no one was in attendance so we had to go downstairs to get our drinks. It also meant that there was no supervision and we could carry on as much as we liked without offending anyone. We split up into pairs and started playing while a couple of people went down to bring us jugs of beer that were all at discount club prices.

We were very happy with our new premises and made a pact to keep it secret from the other punks so that they would have no chance to smash it up and ruin it for us as had happened at Rags. The secret soon spread as secrets will. We soon had forty or fifty punks turning up each night to try their luck on the snooker tables and enjoy the cheap beer. Everyone who attended was sworn to secrecy as we were determined to keep this little piece of paradise to ourselves. Unfortunately, the management was not in on our secret. They soon saw the potential to make more money. The room upstairs was refurbished to incorporate bands with a large stage and even larger bouncers. The Trade Union Club soon became the centre of the rock n' roll scene in Sydney. It remained that way for many years to come but no punk bands ever got to play there.

It is worth mentioning that there were other venues besides Side FX that that were short term venues for Punk. The Oxford Hotel had allowed bands to play in the front bar before it turned gay. The Excelsior did not have bands but did have a great juke box in the front bar and we used to go there to drink and listen to Rock n' Roll classics before it too turned gay. Punk bands rarely played at Frenches and Rejex only played there once from memory. We went there often because it was open late and Big Ray the bouncer would often ask us to leave long after closing. The manager's name was Paul and he was studying at university at the time. He would sometimes sit reading and writing while we sat drinking apple cider until the sun was well and truly up. One of the worst feelings that I can recall is staggering out onto Oxford Street drunk on scrumpies just as the world was waking up. The street was filled with car fumes and the bustle of busy bodies going to work and all we were worried about was getting home before we collapsed.

The best place that we played in terms of a great looking venue was the Paris Theatre. It was an art deco dream that rested on the city side of Hyde Park. It had been a venue for musicals and film in past years and still had the seating and screen for film but had been made redundant by the newer complexes on George Street. It reminded me of Vaudeville and Burlesque and provided the perfect atmosphere for a punk performance. X played a great gig there with one of the biggest inner-city crowds that I ever saw. Johnny Dole and the Scabs also played a comeback gig there with Rejex in support. The Scabs reunion was not a great success. Johnny Dole seemed to be suffering from his lack of success in England. Only those who desired success could suffer from its absence and as the Buddha says, 'desire is the source of all suffering.'

Monique and Michelle's mother also organised a few harbour cruises with punk bands. The ferry cruises weren't really cruises. The ferry would just go to a designated spot in the harbor and park for a few hours. I found the whole thing a bit claustrophobic. The crew found the whole experience terrifying and would lock themselves upstairs to escape our anarchic antics. It was during one of these excursions that the idea of piracy took our imaginations. The idea of hijacking a ferry and taking control of Fort Denison seemed silly but exciting. It was also probably the inspiration for Chaos changing their name to Queen Anne's Revenge when Crasti took over vocals. I don't know if the ferry captain caught wind of our imagined mutiny but we had the water police in a panic and police patrols were soon circling us in the water. When we got back to Circular Quay the whole place was controlled by cops. We had to jump ashore instead of walking the gang plank and escape like rays leaving a sinking ship.

Meanwhile back at Side FX I did have a fight with what I thought was a skinhead on a night when I had snorted a lot of speed. It was not my drug of choice and was something that I did not react to well. I was dancing happily to the Bedhogs when a tall guy with a skinhead haircut started thrashing around in a very aggressive a manner. When the song finished, I turned around to tell him to calm down. He shaped up so I hit him and then I hit him again and again as he seemed to be moving in slow motion. The mixture of speed and adrenaline was so potent that I could have hit him several more times as he was falling to the ground. I felt like I was the king of the world and threw my arms in the air to celebrate my victory. As I was standing there full of myself my old friend Beth spun me around and punched me right in the nose. Even though my head was ringing from the blow I heard her say that I was a bastard because the guy I had hit was having chemotherapy and was dying of cancer. In order to get my head together I went outside to what would have been the school playground. It was a small brick courtyard with several trees surrounded by rings of dirt. There was also a ring of punks surrounding two figures who were facing off ready to fight. One was Terry and the other was a yobbo with long hair and a beard who I had never seen before. He was obviously reluctant to take on Terry and was looking around the crowd for an excuse to escape. When he saw me standing off to the side his eyes lit up. He started yelling that I was the one that did and came toward me at full throttle. I was still shaking from my previous encounter and struggling to figure out what was going on as he grabbed me and dragged me to the ground. Terry thought that it was pretty funny and took his place with the crowd cheering from the sidelines.

The Yobbo was drunk but was also big and strong. We were wrestling on the ground so I couldn't get enough space to throw a punch. I kept trying to get up and he kept dragging me back down. I eventually managed to get on top and straddle him. I started trying to punch him but he kept wrestling. Finally, I decided to pick up a brick. I had no intention of seriously hurting him I just wanted him to lie still. The only thing that saved him and me was that every time I got hold of the brick, he would wrestle around enough to make me drop it. When I dropped the brick, I would punch him again and try to reach for the brick. This kept going until he eventually lay still and I had no need of the brick. It took me a couple of days to come down off the speed and for the possible consequences of my almost action to sink in. I knew that I would never have hit a guy with a brick no matter how drunk or angry I was. There was no malicious intent just a seemingly rational response to an unsatisfactory situation. Remembering how cold blooded the thought process was left me in a cold sweat for several days. It was a miracle that I didn't murder him. The whole night did go to show that you can feel like hero even though you are the villain, life can be funny like that!

CHAPTER 18

The Rock Gardens on William Street was the last big place that we played in the early period of punk rock era in Sydney. The Rock Gardens was next door to a Disco called the Zoo. It was a cocaine castle that Donny Sutherland advertised on his late-night television show. It was a hangout for soap stars, second-rate celebrities and low-level gangsters. These were not the type of people to pick fights with punks. There was never any strife on the streets like there had been with Studs. The first few times that we went to the Rock Gardens we had to sneak in the rear entrance which was our usual way. One or two punks would pay and make their way to the back door. We would then sneak in two or three at a time. The bar staff didn't know because they had nothing to do with the door. The bouncers never noticed because they were always on the front door. Once we had befriended the bouncers we always got in for free. The bouncers at the Rock Gardens were named Gary and Frank. Gary was big and blonde with muscles on his muscles. He was an ex-panther from Penrith. He understood our poverty and got paid the same whether we paid or not. Frank was an even bigger bloke with an even bigger reputation. He had a flat top hair do and a totally fearless disposition. He was a Kiwi and a career criminal. He was a notorious stand over man around the Cross. He became a short-term celebrity when he had appeared as a wrestler on a television commercial.

The Rock gardens was a weirdly designed space for a live music venue which is probably why it did not last that long. You entered down a flight of stairs on the right-hand side of the building into a large room with a bar to the left. Tables and chairs were spread randomly around the rest of the room. This was a huge area and was largely a waste of space. It was like hanging out in an aircraft hangar. The room where the bands played was entered through double doors around to the left. This space was only half the size of the first room. It had a large stage to the right and tiered seating to the left. It seemed much more suited for live theatre or film. There was a small band room to the right of the stage and a dance floor out front with a polished timber floor that was very slippery when wet. When punks discovered this, it became the custom to wet the dance floor whenever visiting bands played. We would then sit in the tiered seat and watch people slip and slide all over the place like they were on skates.

Rejex were being sort of managed by Mr. Suit from the Thought Criminals at this time. He booked us for several gigs as the support act for visiting overseas bands. This was nice but ultimately pointless as we had no plans of joining the mainstream. There was one particular night when he booked as the support act for a band called Wild West. No one had ever heard of this band. They were friends of Rogers' and he probably thought that they had potential. We resented being relegated to the support act when we still pulling pretty big crowds on our own. I decided to raise my concerns with Roger at the bar before we played. He was then going out with a girl named Rowan who was friends with Dorothy and the sister of the original punk princess Jessica. Rowan a was spoiled private school girl who believed that she was now queen of the scene. She was standing next to Roger when I approached and interrupted me by saying 'band whinge' over and over again. This was so annoying that I pushed her away and she fell hard on her behind. This bruised Roger's ego more than it bruised Rowena's backside.

We played the support that night and it ended up being one of our best gigs. The place was full of punks and we did three encores before finishing exhausted but exultant. We sat in the band room afterwards smoking joints and celebrating our success. We kept sneaking looks onstage to laugh at just how badly Roger's proteges were performing. All of the punks had retired to the outside lounge and just a few fanatical followers were left. They tried to lift the spirits of their friends by cheering every song but it just made the whole scene seem even more pathetic. Roger came into the band room to congratulate us and Charley offered him a joint. He took the proffered reefer reluctantly and said that it reminded him of his younger days which made us all laugh out loud. He managed the situation by not managing the situation and he never booked us again.

The other notable thing about the Rock Garden was that it hosted Mod Night Out. The great thing about Mod Night Out was that there were never any mods there. It was held on a Wednesday night because they didn't have the numbers to support a weekend gig and because there weren't many mod bands. I can't remember who actually played but they were always unpleasantly surprised to find that the place filled with punks. Mod Night Out became the biggest punk night out for the several weeks that it lasted. We would first gather at the Outback Bar in the Cross at happy hour where we would load up on Black Russians, Tequila Sunrises and anything else that was on offer. We would then buy flasks of spirits to smuggle into the club to mix with the free soft drinks that were available to the members of bands. We would triumphantly down William Street singing punk songs in a symbolic display of unity and strength. Gary and Frank were always pleased to see us and would stand aside to allow us to march down the stairs in our farcical formation.

We would always get there early on mod night because Gary and Frank had asked us to avoid any trouble outside the club. This meant that we had to get there before the mods. When the mods finally did arrive the first thing that they would do was to ask the bouncers if there were any punks inside. Gary and Frank would always reply in the affirmative and even exaggerate our numbers in order to intimidate the hapless mods. The mods would then wait outside with their scooters all night rather than risk a coming in and causing a confrontation. This was bad for the bands because they would inevitably get covered in soft drink and saliva or ignored all together if they were lucky. The arrangement worked well for punks and the bouncers as we enjoyed a good night out and they avoided having to do any work. We would always wait for the mods to leave before making our exit to ensure that there was no trouble out on the street afterwards.

The mutual respect between publicans, bouncers and punks that had existed since the very first days with Fred at the Grand Hotel. Gary and Frank were like our older uncles and we considered them friends. Our friendship with Frank came to an end one night when the club was raided by the police. The place filled up quickly with over a dozen detectives supported by at least twenty cops in uniform. Punks headed for the back door in order to escape or the toilets in order to flush their drugs. It took some time for us to realise that they were only there to arrest Frank. He came down the stairs with his arms spread wide to show that he was not armed. The cops kept their distance and circled him slowly, shouting at him to surrender. There were no tasers at the time so they either had to shoot him or tackle him. There were too many witnesses for the first option and not enough courage for the second. The standoff seemed to go on for forever and Frank was obviously feeding off their fear. A couple of the cops then nervously drew their guns and started waving them around. The situation was now getting dangerous for everybody involved. Frank reluctantly resigned and put his hands behind his back. The cops cuffed him and led him back up the stairs acting like they had captured Satan himself.

It was also around this time that I decided to sell my soul to Satan. I was not selling it for fame or fortune or for anything else in particular. I just needed to resolve a situation that had begun with a conversation with my Sister. We both happened to be home at my parents at the same time. We went for a walk around the streets and talked for hours. She told me about a conversation that she had had with someone at college that she couldn't quite remember and couldn't quite describe only that it was spiritual in nature. We decided that because she had been solicited by some stranger through some strange conversation and that she had then spoken to me in a similarly strange conversation that I was therefore meant to meet some stranger in order to have another strange conversation that would then somehow make sense of the whole thing. We were both taking a large amount of drugs at the time so it was not surprising that we made no sense but sibling sense. We were like two detectives trying to solve a crime that had not yet been committed. I went away from my parent's place determined to have a strange conversation with a stranger in order to make spiritual sense of my life. This was even stranger because I had been an avowed atheist since the age of about seven when I had decided that if God was love then it was clear from the way of the world that God could not possibly exist.

I took a copy of the Bible from my parents' house and began asking people in the house at Fitzroy Street what they thought it meant. Fat Chris didn't care and Jimmy's little sister Bin was much too shy to comment. I soon got frustrated and decided that if God would not tell me what was going on then I might as well offer my services to the other side. The logic was that if I could prove that the Devil existed then the opposite would also be true. A few nights later Rejex played at the Rock Gardens and it was one of the craziest nights that I can remember. Mark Suicide Squad had gone around putting Spanish fly in the girl's glasses. There were not many punks present because it was a middle of the week gig. There still would have been forty or fifty people, including Sexy Sue, who was apparently sleeping with Joel's boyfriend at the time. A catfight soon started and the ensuing pandemonium distracted from our performance so much that we decided to stop playing all together.

I told the crowd that it was about time that they entertained us as we had been entertaining them for years. I offered the musical instruments to the audience as I stepped down from the stage. We then sat in the front row and rolled joints while we watched the lunatics take over the asylum. There was a mad rush for the stage with all the girls fighting over who would play what instrument. Several girls grabbed the microphone and managed to make the most awful cacophony imaginable. We all thought that it was pretty funny but a couple of private school girls decided that it was proof that I was the embodiment of pure evil. They stood around our table screaming that I was the Devil. They were convinced that the girls were acting under my spell. At least I had gotten some kind of strange response and any proof of spiritual power no matter how strange still confirmed of the existence of something strange.

The next week I was hanging out in the hangar with Jimmy Bedhog and Fat Chris. They had a fairly regular and ridiculous repartee and I had a hard time getting a word in edgewise. During a lull in the laughter Jimmy turned to me and said that he had something important to talk to me about. I told him to talk to Chris instead because I wasn't in the mood. He insisted that he wanted to talk to me and said that we should go back to his place. I told him that there was no way we could lose Chris. Jimmy told me to wait while he went and had a word with Gary the bouncer. He came back and told Chris that they were going to play a game. He had borrowed Gary's handcuffs and fastened them to the leg of the table. Jimmy could talk anyone into anything. He somehow convinced Chris into putting his wrist inside the other cuff. We left the club and went back to Jimmy's place on Burton Street while Chris tried to break the table and make his escape.

We listened to Gene Vincent records and drank long necks until Jimmy found the time and the nerve to speak up. He then looked me straight in the eyes and said 'God exists.' I was taken aback to say the least. My strange conversation with a stranger had just become even stranger. I could have told him about the weirdness of the last few weeks but I didn't even understand it myself. I asked how he could be so sure. Jimmy refused to comment further. No matter how much I badgered him he kept insisting that I needed to talk to his sister Bin. I told him that I had already asked her about such matters and had spent several long and unproductive evenings reading passages of the Bible to her. Jimmy said that she was only being shy and that I should tell her that I had already spoken to him about it. I was forced to wander home in the dark.

When I got back to Fitzroy Street I went straight up to Bin's bedroom and told her to wake up. She was reluctant to get out of bed but I told her that Jimmy had said that I had to talk to her so she had better start talking. She reluctantly got dressed and came down stairs carrying a stack of papers that she insisted would explain everything. I was in no mood to read and did not have either the patience or sobriety to comply. I eventually convinced her to describe everything that had happened so far. She first prefaced her story by saying that I would think that she was crazy. I told her that that was normal around here. She said that Jimmy had been healed of his lymphoma by God and that her mother and her mother's twin sister Tony had been attending Catholic charismatic meetings where they had also received messages about the end of the world.

She was relieved to find that I was not surprised but only relieved to be told what was going on. She explained that she thought I was only joking when I had read the Bible to her. She thought that I was trying to trick her into confessing her belief so that we could burn her at the stake as a punk heretic. I must admit that it was a lot of pressure for a sixteen-year-old girl from the bush to bare and that I probably would have mocked her faith if it had happened a few weeks earlier. Our mutual relief soon outweighed our shared insecurities. The strange circumstances finally started to make some strange sense even if that sense was strangely spiritual. Even my harshest critics should forgive this catholic turn of events considering the confluence of events. A wise man once said that coincidence is the corner stone of fate. I did not realise that I was talking about myself when I wrote this.

It was not long before Fat Chris arrived home having been finally freed from the handcuffs. Bin and I continued our conversation as Chris sat sipping a cup of tea. He looked like he was listening to a foreign language. After a while his frustration got the better of him and he jumped out of his seat asking why we wouldn't tell him what was going on. We told him that we weren't telling him what was going on in case he thought that we were mad. This made him mad and he was soon as anxious as I had been to find out what was going on. He assured us that he would not think that we were mad so we told him to stop him from being so mad. He sat for several seconds trying to figure out whether we were serious or whether we were just setting him up for another prank. When he finally understood that we were sincere he jumped off the couch and said that he was going to tell Rob Millionaire. Rob lived just two houses up the road. Chris was already spreading the news before we had time to stop him. Rob turned out to be just as receptive as Chris and miraculously did not seem to question the idea of a miracle at all.

The revelation reminded me of one afternoon when we had all sat around smoking cones. We were drinking tea and talking with the stereo playing and the sound turned down on the television. Everyone's eyes were soon drawn toward the television screen and a strange silence came upon us as Dr Strangelove took control of the lounge room. The power of Kubrick's art and the message that he was delivering was far more potent than our punk poses and touched the nerve of our collective sub conscious concerns. We turned down the stereo and turned up the atomic explosions and as the mushroom clouds filled the screen. We tacitly acknowledged that this was the reason that we were all here. The realisation that the Sex Pistols cry of no future might well have been more prophetic than we liked to imagine. That punk was the final scream of horror in the face of possible nuclear annihilation. We also laughed along with Peter Sellers over our cups of tea as we knew that this was the only rational response to such overwhelming anxiety. The apocalyptic messages that Bin carried confirmed these concerns. Although there were no specifics about what was supposed to happen the point was apparent. Regardless of the place of punk on the planet the planet itself was apparently in peril.

On the whole the whole miraculous experience caused hardly a ripple in the punk pond. We were not filled with evangelical zeal or driven to preach conversion to the punk population. We were more impressed by the idea that we needed to convert the rest of the population to punk. People became aware of what we were doing but as we were not totally sure what we doing ourselves it made little difference to the way that we behaved. There were some rumours circulating about Bin casting a spell on me. There was gossip that the two of us were using magic to create a cult following like the Manson family. In reality it was all so ordinary that nothing could have been further from the truth. Jimmy was still alive and that was all that really mattered. As far as he was concerned nothing needed to change. I once asked him what he would do if the world was about to end. He said that he would do exactly what he was doing now. We were proud to be punks and now believed that God was on our side.

CHAPTER 19

The Sydney scene had become so large in the early eighties that it now encompassed all kinds of musical styles. There were mods and rockers and skinheads and punks and everything in between. The Bedhogs had split up and reformed as the Kelpies with Bam Bam from Suicide Squad back on bass and a big bear of a boy named Ashley on drums. There was also a young punk guitar player from Local Product called Brian replacing Little Stewart on rhythm guitar. Little Stewart had moved on and joined Sydney's first ska band called the Allniters. They were formed by a guy named Martin, and Hoody the Kiwi who shared Stewarts love of reggae. English bands like Madness and the Specials had started this scene and people were now keen for anything new and different. Many people who had been too young to be members of the punk scene wanted to be sure that they did not miss out this time. There was a mad scramble to be amongst the first to ride the new wave. New Wave was also the term that the mainstream media was now using to transform punk into a more palatable product.

The changes in the scene were no more evident than when we went to see a new mod band called the Cockroaches at a club in Newtown one night. We had been invited by a kid called Phil who was playing the bass and had been a member of the early punk scene. The room was filled with rich young things eager to impress. It took me a while to adjust to the atmosphere because it was so different to anything that I had seen in the scene before. There is a certain arrogance that comes with wealth because there is no fear of failure. Your fate is not dependent on your talent but on the security of sound financial foundations. It was just as well that the cockroaches weren't depending on their talent because it was conspicuously absent that night. Members of the band later went on to study child phycology. They did not do this to improve the mental well-being of children. They did this to learn how to manipulate their minds in order to make money. I know that it is not good to judge people but I really hope the Wiggles burn in hell!

Rejex still had a large and loyal following but the gigs had dried up after my confrontation with Roger at the Rock Gardens. He was now making money out of the new wave with bands like the Machinations. In order to emphasise the fact that things had changed the universe got us a gig at the Grand Hotel with the Allniters. The people who purchased the Grand had renovated and tried to turn the place into a restaurant. The two front bars had been tarted up with tiles and a coat of paint. The backroom had been turned into a background for a Specials film clip with black and white checks everywhere. It suited the Allniters perfectly but made us feel instantly awkward. It was so strange playing in that place with rude boys decorating the back wall. It was even stranger to see the faces of the punks present and realise that we did not know them personally. The scene and the band had gone full circle from ritual to spectacle. The cynicism and sneers from the ska boys was a stark contrast to the uniform celebrations of our punk past. The gig perfectly symbolized the sad passing of our punk paradise.

We went to the pool room after we finished playing feeling a little stunned and stale. The sense that the scene had changed was so certain that we needed no words. It also set the scene for the final curtain to be closed on our career. Richard had been dating an English girl for some time and the situation had become serious. She objected to him spending so much time with us and had cried and carried on the last time we had rescued him for rehearsal. She was looking for an excuse to break up the band and this gig had provided the perfect platform. There was a genuine feeling of grief in the air and no real doubt that the dance was over. No matter how hard it was to acknowledge the end there were no hard feelings. We shook hands with heavy hearts and left with no lack of love. It had been a wild ride with never a doubt or dull moment. We later attended Richard's wedding at the Wayside chapel but this was the funeral when we buried the band.

The house in Fitzroy Street closed soon after the band folded. We sat on the verandah smoking hash oil donated by Mad Mick while we waited to move. Mick was Ross Guerilla's brother and was living on the roof of a nearby disused building with a bunch of cats. The cats used to follow him around like dogs and would often turn up before him as if announcing his arrival. We were listening to Sticky Fingers and watching a guy named Cowboy move in across the street. Cowboy was the new drug dealer in town. He drove a gold Trans Am with a peroxided blonde as a necessary accessory. The fact that he could be so obvious about his profession made us think that he had drug squad connections. He would soon be one of the first people to start pushing heroine in the scene. The move to replace the pot supply with something much harder was supported by some very well connected and well-respected Sydney celebrities. Cowboy started making a lot more money but it only made him want more money. He ended in an alleyway in Rushcutters Bay with two clips from an automatic emptied into him.

After the house on Fitzroy Street finished, I moved to Woomera Avenue for a while. I got a job With Pommy Ian at a fiber glass factory out near Botany Bay. The top floor was a furnace that liquified the fiber glass so the factory was as hot as hell. The liquid would then cool and be broken into chips which would be funneled into bags. Our job was to stack the bags on a palate and bash them with a bat. It was so dusty inside you couldn't see six feet in front of you and so noisy that you couldn't hear someone screaming in your ear. On the bus trip home all of the factory workers would yell at each other because of their industrial deafness. Occupational health and safety wasn't big in the seventies or early eighties. We didn't last there long and I decided to move home to Wentworthville for a while in order to recover.

WARNING: All those who object to reading the gospels should close their eyes now. For all those with their eyes still open, I spent the next few months recovering and reading the Bible. I discovered that Christian theology had a lot in common with punk philosophy. The idea that you could not worship God and money, that you would love one and despise the other (Mat 6:24) was similar to our rejection of main stream success. Jesus smashing up the moneylender's tables may not have been the same as our destroy parties but the principle against profit was similar (Mat 21: 12,13). The idea that Christians should be passive and peaceful is also undermined by Jesus when he says 'Do not suppose that my mission on earth is to spread peace. My mission is to spread, not peace, but division' (Mat 10:34). There is also the part about it being harder for a rich man to enter the kingdom of heaven than for a camel to pass through the eye of a needle (Mat 19:24). And, 'woe to the rich, for your consolation is now' (Luke 6:24). Capitalism and Christianity are clearly mutually exclusive ideologies in the New Testament. Heaven does not appear to be a place for those who are well liked or super successful either when Jesus asks, 'if you find that the world hates you know that it has hated me before you. If you belonged to the world, it would love you as its own; the reason it hates you is that you do not belong to the world. But I chose you out of the world (John 15:18,19).' The quest for fame and fortune is also questioned when Jesus asks, 'What profit does a man show if he were to gain the whole world and destroy himself in the process (Mat 16:26)?' The rejection of the world and prevailing political and social principles seems to be a prerequisite for paradise. The gospels seem to say that being a rebel is required while accepting and participating in the current mainstream consumer culture is a mistake, as Jesus tells us to, 'enter through the narrow gate. The gate that leads to damnation is wide, the road is clear, and many choose to travel it. But how narrow is the gate that leads to life, how rough the road, and how few there are who find it (Mat 7:13,14)! The fact that Jesus was crucified as a criminal for speaking the truth reflected our own treatment at the hands of the police. The only person to be promised paradise was the criminal crucified on the cross beside Jesus. He was not a Christian or a Jew he only recognized and spoke the truth (Luke 24:40,43). In order to follow The Christian path, you were expected to give up all of your worldly possessions and you had to do the same to be a punk even though most of us did not have worldly possessions to give up in the first place (Mat 19:21). You had to give up your past life and your former beliefs in order to be reborn as a punk or as a Christian (Mat 16:25), 'The community of believers were of one heart and one mind. None of them ever claimed anything as his own; rather, everything was held in common' (Acts 4: 32). That contemporary Christians seem to believe that they can be comfortably middle class and still look forward to salvation seems to be at odds with the teachings of the New Testament. The Capitalist zeal of the American evangelicals is diametrically opposed to the lives of the Apostles in Acts. My favourite story is when the Apostle Peter confronts a man called Ananias who has sold his property in order to join the Christian community but keeps a portion of the proceeds:

'Peter exclaimed; "Ananias why have you let Satan fill your heart so as to make you lie to the Holy Spirit and keep for yourself some of the proceeds from that field? Was it not yours so long as it remained unsold? Even when you sold it, was not the money still yours? How could you ever concoct such a scheme? You have lied not to men but to God!" At the sound of these words, Ananias fell dead.' (Acts 5:3,4,5)

The major difference between the Christian and punk paths seemed to be that Christians are promised paradise while punks had no chance of being rewarded by anyone at any time. In one way perhaps punk was the purer path. My father grew concerned when he noticed my newly found fervour for the Bible. He asked me if I intended joining the priesthood. I thought that this was pretty funny and told him that I still had no intention of being anything other than a punk. If I did have any evangelical zeal it was to convert Christians to Punk rather than the other way around. I had always wanted to try and bring Punk to the suburbs but could never find anyone who supported the idea. Most people had found punk as a way of escaping from suburbia and had no intentions of going back. **NOTICE: You can open your eyes now.**

It was while I was living at my parent's house that I saw Vonnie for the last time. Our paths had crossed for a brief time at Rags when Rejex ruled. We had spent time at Australia Street together on occasion. I can't remember where or how we met this time, only that she rode back on the train with me to Wentworthville and stayed the night in my sister's old bedroom. The look on my parents faces when they saw her the next morning was priceless. Vonnie appeared as both an innocent child and an indolent whore, eating her breakfast cereal with so much sugar she was like a succubus with a sweet tooth. My parents left the house for work but probably spent the rest of the day ringing around for an exorcist. The only reason that we did not share a room was because she had told me the night before that she was married. The wicked witch had been wed and the magic had disappeared from the relationship just as it had disappeared from the scene itself.

After breakfast we went out into the back garden to drink tea and talk. It could have been the most wonderful day of my life but my fairy from the ferry had proven to be a mere mortal after all. It was the first time since I had known her that I did not desire her utterly. It was a day that you look back on with mixed feelings and a bitter sweet taste no matter how you try to flavour the memory in your mind. The worst thing about the experience was that Vonnie spent the entire day trying to get into my pants. My body was screaming at me to take her but my mind was screaming no! Each time my resistance weakened She would pull away and giggle mischievously. It was more that she wanted me to desire her rather any real intention of consummation. I either had to force the issue or forsake any further thought of physical satisfaction. To say that it was the hardest day of my life so far would be too terrible a pun. After many cups of tea between bouts of cat and mouse, I doubled her back to Wentworthville Station on the back of my push bike. I do remember that there was a dog wandering the platform looking for water and I turned on the tap so that he could drink. Vonnie smiled and said that we were too similar to be anything more than friends. We then sat in silence until the train arrived and I never saw her again.

The only other person that came to visit me in my exile was Jamie Jetson. She rang me up one night out of the blue. She told me that she had talked some guy into driving her out to the suburbs by telling them that I was her long-lost brother. I told her not to come to the house because my parents were still too freaked out from the from the visit from Vonnie. She pulled up out the front and I went out to meet her and her besotted boyfriend. Jamie was dressed like Adam Ant as Ant Music was then number one on the charts. Her companion was a very straight looking salesman type dressed in a suit. Jamie jumped from the car to greet me and smothered me in hugs and kisses. It was far too sensual for a sibling but I still called her sis and told her to get back in the car. We drove to the local pub and her friend waited like a faithful puppy in the car while we went in to have a beer. I put Ant Music on the jukebox and watched Jamie shake her stuff on the beer stained carpet much to the delight of the beer bellied patrons. They would have been willing to pay good money for such a performance. Jamie received a warm round of applause and took a bow before she sat down.

She then filled me in on all the gossip and asked me why the hell I was where I was. I told her all about Jimmy and explained that I didn't really want to be where I was but it was what it was. She wanted me to go back in to town with her and stay at her place. I was tempted but knew that living with someone as crazy as Jamie would inevitably make me crazy too. She told me that I should get the band back together or give up music forever. I told her that this wasn't going to happen. She told me to start another band and I knew that she was right. I had always wanted to bring punk to the suburbs and although Jamie had made a fair impression, I needed music to complete the mission. She was such a sweet soul and like Vonnie she had a childlike quality that was totally at odds with her outward appearance. She was a wonderful girl and it did my heart good just to see her. We eventually finished drinking and she got her friend to drive me home. When we arrived, I explained to the chauffeur that we weren't really brother and sister just to see what he would say. I wanted to make sure that he wouldn't get upset and turn violent once I was gone. He insisted that he didn't care and his lovelorn look convinced me that he was obsessed and totally under her spell. It was a mad night and reminded me of my own mad love for the city and all the mad people there. I needed another band to start my evangelical adventure of bringing punk to the wider population and I could only do this by going back into town. Sometimes you need to see someone crazy to see what is sane, life can be funny like that!

CHAPTER 20

My exile finally ended when I was invited to share a house in the Baker's Dozen in Palmer Street with Wendy and Shirley. The Baker's Dozen was a block of thirteen identical terraces that were painted all orange at the time. You walked into a hall with a bedroom on the left and a large lounge at the end. You then walked through to the kitchen which had one wall of glass that looked across to the kitchen next door. There was another three bedrooms and a bathroom upstairs. There must have been a few more people living there but I can't remember who. I do remember that everyone in the house was working and Little Rob was also over all the time because he was going out with Wendy. Rob had converted the girls to the occult and they spent their time casting spells.

Our house was next to the end of the row and was almost opposite a squat called the compound. This was a social scene within itself on the edge of the city and on the edge of straight society. It was a sprawling structure that took up two blocks and the whole place lent to the left. It was like entering Aladdin's cave with niches and nooks everywhere separated by colourful curtains and carefully considered tie dyed clothe. There was an aura of eastern religion and an excess of Persian rugs. There was a separate space set aside for performance with a small stage and ramshackle seating spread randomly about the room. No one from there ever seemed to perform publicly. It was like a secret self-contained time capsule stuck in the sixties. It was just one example of the spread of separate and surprising sub cultures that started in the late seventies. There was no longer any real uniformity to rebellion, only separate cells spread all over the city scape. This has been the problem with the Sydney scene since the seventies, everyone thinks that their sect is special so no one supports anyone else.

The only special person to enter our scene at the time was the Spooner monster. The Spooner monster was a pale, smooth skinned kid whose teeth seemed to be too big for his mouth. He had faded blonde hair and big bright blue eyes that made him look like he was permanently excited about something. He also had two scars down his back from a lung operation that made it appear as if he were a fallen angel that had had its wings removed. He had first fallen to earth at the Stage Door Tavern in a Day-Glo suit with fluorescent rings around it like he was a spaceman who had lost his ship. He had hung around with the trendies at Stranded disco and had been bisexual before embracing the punk culture which was still a very straight scene. He had become very excited when he had heard about Jimmy and wanted to convert. The whole conversion thing was proving to be pretty complex. There was some consternation about the Spooner monsters' motivation. He was easily led and had always wanted to fit in with what he thought was the cool crowd. His sense of celebrity was also questionable as he certainly did worship Jimmy.

Little Rob knew a lot more about religion than I did and we had a number of conversations on the subject that where very helpful. On one occasion we all went up to celebrate Spooner's twenty first birthday at his parent's house. I introduced Rob to their family's priest and they sat together out in the garden having a very long conversation that they both seemed to enjoy very much. This would have seemed weird if you didn't know Rob very well but he had the most open mind of anyone I knew at the time. At another time he did perform a service that proved quite providential on a quiet afternoon at Palmer Street. The Spooner Monster and I were just sitting around being bored when Rob appeared with his tarot cards and offered to do a reading. The Spooner Monster sat down with his big toothed grin and puppy like enthusiasm while Rob shuffled the cards.

It was like watching psychic surgery. Rob's reading was so precise and personnel the Spooner's enthusiasm was soon transplanted by anxiety and the big cheeky grin was replaced by a grimace. The precision of Rob's reading may well have been a result of his own keen insight. The criticism may have been a reflection of his personnel views on Christian conversion but this did not make his insights any less truthful. He dissected the Spooner Monster's motivation and commitment while chipping away at the façade of his childlike faith. They say that the truth hurts and I sat cringing at every cut of the spiritual scalpel. When Little Rob was finished the sun was setting and he got up to turn on the light. Paul sat still with his head bowed, obviously feeling bruised by the experience. He finally looked up and saw that the shape of a fish was being cast by the light shade onto the ceiling. The childlike glee was back in an instant as he pointed out that the fish was used as a symbol for Christ amongst early Christians. He jumped to his feet and danced around the room as if he had not suffered from the surgery at all. He was then quickly put back in his place when Little Rob reminded him who had actually turned the light on.

It was also during my time at Palmer Street that I was taken to a most interesting restaurant. My guide was a guy named Aaron. He was an effeminate inner-city kid who had olive skin, short black hair and big brown eyes. If he were around today everyone would have assumed that he was gay but Aaron had a girlfriend. His girlfriend's name was Tessa. She was a pretty girl with slightly freckled skin and even bigger brown eyes. Neither of them looked like punks. They were part of the new breed who saw life as a smorgasbord and tasted whatever suited their palate at the time. They took me down to a house near Bill and Tony's café on Burton Street in Woolloomooloo. The house was an unlicensed restaurant called Slys or the hole in the wall depending on who you talked too. There were itinerant Italian workers hanging around on the footpath outside and we waited with them until the place opened. The opening time was announced by a rotund middle-aged Italian woman who leant out of the backdoor and yelled something in Italian in a really loud voice. We all shuffled up the back stairs and through the kitchen into a large lounge room that had been expanded by knocking down an adjoining wall. The space was filled with tables and chairs that were soon filled with ravenous middle-aged Italian men. There were free bread rolls on the table and a choice of free homemade wine or lemonade. There was a variety of pasta meals on offer and the whole experience cost just two dollars. The children of the owners waited on the tables. They had little patience for non-Italians and served the food with a marvelous mixture of deference and disdain. They soon took objection to the greedy way we disposed of the free house wine. Aaron argued with them with an enviable familiarity while they stole his cutlery and took away his glass. It was like a free floorshow to go with the free wine and bread. We were being out punked by these local juvenile delinquents whose hospitality had clearly defined limits. It was a wonderful dining experience.

This was just one of many such places that were provided by the local Maltese and Italian communities that shared Woolloomooloo. They were there to support the itinerant labourers who were largely single men. They all sent a portion of their incomes home to help their extended families overseas and had probably been doing so since the second world war. There was also a place called No Names just around the corner. No Names was in a much larger house and trendies soon replaced the Italians. It later attempted to become a main stream pasta chain when it opened a place in Norton Street. There was also a place called Garibaldis at the bottom of Riley Street that served Italian food. It was a favourite hangout for socialists and also served as a music venue on occasion. The Astoria and the New Yorker in Kings Cross also offered really good meals for less than five dollars. These were the last places in the inner city that still had a strong sense of civic duty. They were there to serve the needs of the local community and always put their patrons before their profit. I still savour the flavor of these restaurants in my memory as they remind me of a side of Sydney that has been thrown out with the scraps.

Such excursions and the company of good friends were important to me as I had decided to give up drugs and fighting. It turned out that I had only given up buying drugs and quickly folded as soon as someone offered them to me. The giving up fighting was easy as long as I avoided the drink and the surrounding circumstances. One of these surrounding circumstances did occur when I was walking home down Palmer Street one day. A scary looking character with disheveled clothes and an obviously even more disheveled mind stopped me and asked me if I was Johnny Rejex. I responded in the affirmative and he said that he had once seen me waste a guy with my bare hands and now he was going to waste me. I stood frozen waiting to see what he was going to do. He wasn't physically intimidating but the craziness made me think twice. I was waiting to see what kind of weapon he had. I was thinking that if I ran and he had a gun he could shoot me in the back. If I stayed still and waited, I might be able to grab the gun. If he had a knife I could just run away or try to take it from him. The indecision kept me glued to the spot. After what seemed like ages and when he did not display a weapon or make a move I asked him how he was going to waste me. He adopted a martial arts pose and stretched out his hands saying 'with these.' I was so wound up by now that I could have killed him on the spot. The only thing that saved him was his girlfriend. She came running down the road in the nick of time screaming and waving her arms in a panic. She begged me not to hurt him and explained that he had been on speed for six weeks and had no idea what he was doing. I told her to take him home and lock him up in his room until he was sane. I said that if I saw him on the streets again, I wouldn't wait to see a weapon before I killed him. I was still shaking when I got home but I never saw the guy again.

The other occasion that severely tested my newfound peace and sobriety was when the people next door had a party. The opposing kitchens on the ground floor meant that you could see straight across into the neighbours' kitchen through the large side windows. On this particular night it was like looking into a particularly debauched level of Dante's Inferno. There seemed to be more bottles being broken than being drunk. While they were getting drunk and ridiculous, we were being sober and serious while drinking tea. We made stupid jokes about how T-riffic out t-shirts were while the house opposite descended further into furor. Some people in the opposite kitchen soon noticed our relative bliss and came across to see what drugs we were on. They found it very difficult to accept that we were just drinking tea and insisted upon a forensic examination of the teapot and the leaves before they would leave.

A fun night was had by all who were not at the party and I went to bed when the noise died down. I was woken up a few hours later by Terry the Doorman calling my name from the backyard. The call was soon accompanied by a loud banging on the back door so I went down and see what the trouble was. Terry was barely standing and was obviously in a bad mood. He told me that his Girlfriend Donna had been kicked out of the party next door. He wasn't at the party because he had been working a door in the Cross at the time. He had come to teach them a lesson and wanted me to watch his back. I told him that I wasn't fighting anymore and that he was too drunk to do anything anyway. Terry would not be deterred and I couldn't say no to a friend in need.

We went over to the house next door and Terry went straight in through the unlocked kitchen door. He started shouting out for the person who was responsible for Donna's earlier eviction. After several moments there was some scurrying on the stairs and four blokes came down to confront us in the kitchen. I realised that there wasn't much room for Terry to throw his punches and that he would soon be overwhelmed by sheer numbers. I managed to grab him and drag him out the back door before they could get hold of him. They all fell out of the door after us and were so drunk that they ended up sprawled all over the ground. The guy that Terry was after was named Adam and he was first to his feet. The other three were struggling with Terry on the ground. Adam seized his opportunity and got ready to kick Terry in the head. I wasn't sure what to do, I just knew that I had to do something. I was so frustrated by the situation that I just yelled out 'NO!" with all of my considerable lung power. Everyone was so shocked by the sound that they stopped long enough for Terry to get to his feet.

The mixture of fresh air and adrenaline soon sobered Terry up and he was now ready to rumble. The four guys circled him nervously before deciding to rush him. Terry elbowed the guy coming from behind and in one motion punched the guy in front of him. He then flicked out his left hand and caught the guy coming from his side with a clean, perfectly timed jab. Adam was the last man standing and managed to get close enough to grab Terry by the front of the shirt. Terry hit him with a rabbit punch that couldn't have travelled more than six inches but sent Adam flying six feet backwards. The whole thing could only have lasted about six seconds. There were now four bodies sprawled in the back-yard bleeding. Adam then noticed that his front teeth were missing. He got up and started threatening to shoot Terry. He didn't have a gun so we ignored him and went inside to have a cup of tea.

CHAPTER 21

My time in the Baker's Dozen and my attempted abstinence were soon over. Rob Millionaire, Fat Chris, Nick Sleaze and the Spooner Monster had all found a place in Thurlow Street in Redfern and had asked me to move in with them. It was a large two-story terrace with a garage. This meant that we all had separate bedrooms as well as a pool table out the back. It was the first time that I felt a sense of reluctance in regard to such an invitation because I knew the house would be full of hash as well as punks. I did not object to anyone else taking drugs but did feel a need to slow down myself and even try to set some kind of example. I was used to setting an example when it came to madness and mayhem but this was something quite different.

Rob used to get up very early in order to work as a boner at the abattoir. He would generally return home very early in the morning. Fat Chris and I had scored jobs as detailers at a car rental place in Bourke Street just down from Taylor Square. We would be preparing to go to work just when Rob was getting home. The others would often get up early in time to watch the Beverly Hillbillies on television and line up at the stove to have hot knives for breakfast. For those who are not familiar with this particular method of imbibing hashish it involves cutting the bottom off a large plastic drink container. A knife is heated over the stove until it is red hot. A piece of hashish is then placed on the flat surface of another knife that is still cool. The heated knife is then placed on top of the piece of hash. The opened bottom of the plastic container is used to capture the fumes and they are inhaled through the screw top end. The line of people would rotate until everyone had their fill. Everyone else would retire to the lounge while Chris and I walked to work. I did try for a short time not to partake but peer pressure and the seduction of such rituals was far more powerful than my mere will power. We also smoked hash in a bong with tobacco and after walking to work on my own one morning I found that I was overwhelmed by a strange craving. I knew it wasn't for hash because I was already so stoned that my body felt numb. It took me some time to realise that it was the Tobacco that I craved. I went to the shop and purchased my first pack of cigarettes. This was so stupid that I still can't believe that I did it. I ended up adding a new addiction instead of ending my addictions.

The building that we were working in was the old Sergeants pie factory. Our workspace overlooked the backyards next to the Tradesman's Arms Hotel. This pub was as notorious for drugs as the Lord Nelson Hotel had been for whores. The backyards were riddled with narrow lanes that had been used for garbage and sanitary collection not so long ago. Chris and I would watch prospective customers walk up the access alley to knock on a wooden gate. They would then wait anxiously while the dealer on the other side checked them out. We would wait until the transaction was about to take place and then spray them with our hose. Sometimes the people would panic immediately once they knew that they were being watched. Sometimes they would wait and weigh up the score against the idea of being busted. The dealer would always withdraw because they knew that the junkie would soon be back. We found the mixture of desperation and despair to be hilarious. We were careful to do this occasionally and randomly because we didn't want the dealers to catch on.

These were the same guys who had bashed Crasti and Colin Chaos outside the Oxford Hotel. We did not realise that the addiction that we found so funny would soon play a most painful and pathetic part in punk.

Nick and I soon began jamming at the house in Thurlow Street with the Spooner Monster on guitar. Spooner had not played much previously but he soon became proficient. The idea of forming a new band became inevitable. We needed a drummer but Charley had disappeared out West when Rejex split up. It was the first time that I experienced a sense of destiny because I knew that his return was just around the corner. He moved in just around the corner a few weeks later with my original punk companion Craig Jones. We rehearsed in the upstairs bedroom and soon had a set together. We decided that we could not use Rejex as Richard had not returned. The search for a band name is always difficult but we eventually settled on Vellocette. It was used in A Clock Work Orange as the speed supplement in the moloko plus milkshake. It was also the name of one of Charley's favourite motorcycles.

The house at Thurlow Street was also where I celebrated my twenty first birthday. We had a party and even my parents turned up for a short time. This meant that we had to hide all the smoking paraphernalia for a while which made people impatient. My father liked a beer or two himself. He didn't particularly like the people but he had started telling stories and was reluctant to leave. Mum was far less comfortable in the strange surroundings and soon convinced him that he was better off at the bowling club. We were soon lined up at the stove imbibing hash with our hot knives and the party was soon in full swing.

I don't remember much about the party except that it was a good mixture of the old and new. There were a group of young girls there who were following the Spooner Monster around like he was some kind of guru. I do remember some strange guy coming up to sit next to me on the lounge and ask me why I thought that I was so cool. I was extremely out of it and having a wonderful time so I was in no mood for such a stupid question. I was still sticking to my renunciation of violence so I had no idea what to do about it. The guy realized my reluctance and started to badger me more. Just when I was about to break my vow Jimmy turned up to see what was happening. He sat down on the lounge and put his arm around the guy. The guy must have been really drunk or really stupid or both because he did not realise that this was far from a friendly gesture. Jimmy asked me what was happening and I told him what the guy had said. Jimmy was never slow to help a friend or to get involved in violence. He told the guy that I was cool and that jealousy was not a good look. The guy decided to protest so Jimmy hit him in the head. The guy then proved just how stupid he actually was by declaring that it hadn't hurt and that he didn't mind being hit in the head. Just to make sure that he wasn't lying Jimmy leant over and hit him again. The guy started to cry so Jimmy told him to say sorry or he would keep on hitting him in the head. The guy started sobbing and saying he was sorry and generally being pretty pathetic so Jimmy picked him up off the lounge and comforted him all the way to the front door where he threw him out onto the street.

The other thing I remember was that Laura Horizontal turned up with her new skin head boyfriend. Laura had gone out with Lez wreckage for a long time and he had taken their breakup pretty bad. The fact that she was flaunting her new flame right in front of Les did not go down well with his friends. When the skin realized that he was not welcome he started to rave on about how he wasn't scared and that he was going to get his friends to finish us off if we tried anything. He was definitely a downer and was harshing our buzz like a blow fly at a picnic. We decided to offer him up as a sacrifice as part of my birthday celebrations. Bob the boner and the boys bundled him up and dragged him out to the garage.

Ross Meathead grabbed a rope and threw it over a wooden beam in the ceiling. The skinhead started to realise that we were not mucking around and started kicking and screaming. We attached the rope around his neck and started to hall him up into the air. Laura came running from the house and started slapping us as her boyfriend's feet flashed about our heads. It was all becoming too much trouble so we let go of the rope. The skin crashed to the ground before jumping to his feet and running out the back door with the rope still hanging around his neck and Laura chasing after him.

It was also around the time of my twenty first birthday that Les started to use the term Barmy. An English young punk band called Exploited had come out with a song called Barmy Army. Their album seemed to signal a change in the culture from fun and humour to anger and political angst. I did not like the new tone and found no joy in the new music or the new attitude it represented. The term young punk had been used for so long by now that the young punks in the Sydney scene were now considered as old punks. A new term was needed to describe the new generation of punks. I thought that Les was using barmy as a positive way of describing the new generation of punks. He used it in the adjectival sense like groovy and Les was so cool that I did not think that the term was offensive at all. We all started using it as a general descriptive term for everything and anyone involved with Punk in the eighties.

I was made aware of my error one night when we were walking home from the Southern Cross Hotel with a carton of beer. We saw some punks up the road at a party as we crossed Cleveland Street. We went to investigate and discovered a bunch of barmies hanging around out the front of the house. We went inside to see if we knew anyone and were stopped in the hall by a large skinhead. He was standing in the doorway that led to the lounge room. He was refusing to let us enter unless we shook his hand and said that we were his friends. Fat Chris thought that this was pretty funny and started rubbing the skinhead's scalp and snapping his braces against his chest. This obviously stung the skinheads' nipples as well as his pride because he started swinging. Chris had him on the ground in no time and was pounding away with his big sledge hammer hands. I stepped over the bodies and went to see who was out the back of the house. Kiwi Kim was sitting around a table with a bunch of barmies. They all stopped what they were doing when they saw me and started yelling abuse. I was taken aback because I did not understand the grounds of their grievance and had always considered Kiwi Kim as a friend. I stood stunned for a while until Kim finally completed my confusion by explaining that I was a bastard because I called them barmies. I had thought that everyone now used this term so I was still surprised and responded by saying that they were barmies!

They jumped up from the table and started chasing me down the hall. Fortunately, Fat Chris had finished with the skinhead so there was no impediment to my escape and I managed to make it out onto the street. Once there I found Fat Chris and hid behind him laughing at the absurdity of the situation. The barmies were searching for me up and down the footpath. One of them eventually found me and started screaming for his friends. He started trying to grab me so I hit him in the head. I was still aware of my vow of non-violence so I didn't hit him very hard. To my surprise he fell to the ground and started crying. All the other barmies ran over to help him up and started yelling at me. One of them said that I was now an even bigger bastard because I had hit their friend. I told them that I hadn't hit him that hard and helped him to his feet. I asked him what his problem was and he told me that he hated attention. I then recognised him as the singer in one of the new punk bands. I asked him how he could hate attention when he was the singer in a band. He started crying harder and fell back to the ground as if I had hit him again. The situation was so ridiculous that it defied further speech and we took our beer and went home unable to believe how truly barmy the whole scene had become.

It was also around this time, whatever time this was, that Sydney suffered from a strange drought. The hash supply had suddenly dried up. There were many rumours circulating that this was a deliberately constructed manmade disaster. It seemed that the people who had recently taken over the drug trade in Sydney had decided to stop the supply of hashish in order to assist their sales of heroine. Rob was now receiving his supply from the Cowboy. He was bringing us a very inferior product that tasted like chemicals and gave you a headache. It was horrible hash but nowhere near as horrible as the heroine that was about to hit our streets like the black plague.

One day when the cowboy arrived several people disappeared into the front bedroom room like they were sharing a secret. Several of my best friends hit up heroine for the first time on that day. Most of them are dead or still recovering. They came out of the room spinning and spewing and falling on the floor. They told me that they had hit up speed but the lie was so stupid that it almost upset me more than the actual act. They looked like zombies from a b-grade horror film and so sad that I could not stand to look at them. I grabbed the still straight Spooner and we went up the Trade Union Club to drink away our disappointment. We stayed out all night and brought beers back to the garage so we could drink and play pool until dawn. The next day I woke up with a terrible headache but went down stairs certain that all the would-be junkies were feeling worse. I was disappointed to find that they were celebrating and certain that it was the best thing that had ever happened to them.

It was not long before the plague had spread to almost everyone we knew. It was considered cool to hit up like you were dancing with the devil. It was more like dancing with death as all of our conversations soon centered around who had overdosed. There was a young punk couple who had been together for several years. They made everyone sick with their pet names and incessant cuddling and smooching. They had hit up together and soon their addiction to smack became more important than their addiction to each other. One dark night the girl overdosed. Believing that he would be busted the boyfriend got a friend to help him. They carried the body of his dead girlfriend up an alley and threw her over a fence. We had gone from living the dream to living a nightmare in the instant that it takes to mainline. Two of the young girls that had been at my birthday party a few months before were now dead and buried. I took up playing golf to escape the deadly depression that had descended on the house. I would wander over to Moore Park Golf Club and hit balls around in full punk gear to get a giggle. One minute we were living like legends and the next we were surviving in the shadow of death and there was nothing funny about it.

CHAPTER 22

It was not long before the house of heroine fell apart. The members of Vellocette moved to small terrace in Lower Campbell Street that had a skyscraper growing in the backyard. Pieces of the emerging structure were constantly dropping onto our roof but it meant that we could use the front room for rehearsal without any complaints about noise from the neighbors. We were just around the corner from Oxford Street so we spent allot of time drinking at Frenches. We also spent allot of time playing video games on Nicks' new computer. There was a game with two tanks chasing each other around a maze and electronic tennis. These might seem primitive now but it was endlessly fascinating then.

Fortunately, our focus soon shifted when Charley located a hotel at Parramatta called the Royal Oak. He had arranged a deal with the management so that we could use the back room for bands. The pub was directly opposite the War and Peace nightclub which was the largest mainstream venue in the West at the time. The geographical opposition matched our philosophical opposition and meant that our crusade into the suburbs was about to begin. I had talked Charley into the idea of taking punk to the wild west and he agreed completely with my evangelical zeal. He was a good communicator and had talked a lot of the young punk bands into playing there. Charley also soon rented the top half of a large house in Marriott Street Redfern with Craig and it wasn't long before we all moved into the House of Vellocette.

We inhabited the top half of the house in Marriott Street and the bottom half was filled with the possessions of the owners who were away. There was a rope attached to the front door via the bannister on the stairs so you could open the door without walking down. There was a factory to one side of the house so we didn't directly affect anyone's peace and quiet when we rehearsed. When we did play it became a custom for kids to climb up on the factory roof and dance around which was wonderful. The other wonderful thing that happened was when we were at the local shop one day. A customer came up to ask us if we were the ones in the band. We were reluctant to admit it but it was hard to deny considering our clothes and comradery. To our surprise the neighbor was very happy to meet us and told us that we were very good. We had finally made the transition from pure punk to being actual musicians. The enthusiastic support of our straight neighbors was the first really positive thing that had happened for some time.

I should also mention that Charley's best friend Tony was around the house all the time. He had been around the scene since the Section appeared but had never really become a punk. The two of them were like Heckle and Jeckle and would argue about nothing at all for hours on end. It was always difficult to get a word in edgewise when the two of them were together and they could drown out the band when they were in full cry. They also brought with them a guy called Fat Freddy who could yell down the pair of them when he wanted. It was a strange time for me as my westie past and my punk present were now becoming inextricably entwined. It seemed as if the dream of converting the conservative heartland to punk was becoming a reality and we were all very excited at the prospect.

Spooner borrowed his sisters' station wagon and Charley chipped in with his panel van and the punk caravan hit the road once more. We would pile as many punks as we could into the vehicles and drive down Parramatta road each weekend to spread the word. It was the perfect escape from the death and depression that had enveloped the city scene and gave us a new positive perspective. The gigs at the Royal Oak went really well. It was weird looking out a crowd clad in T-shirts and jeans and long hair. It was very reminiscent of the early days at the Grand with Johnny Dole and the Scabs. The kids in the crowd were very enthusiastic and often thanked me for bringing the culture to them because they would never have ventured into the city themselves.

I remember on one occasion travelling back into town with a whole bunch of westies on board. Both vehicles were filled with the bands gear as well as so many bodies that limbs were hanging out of the car. It was a travelling party that was also reminiscent of the trips around the city in the early days of the Native Rose. On this occasion our party was prevented from reaching its' destination by the intervention of the local Parramatta police. They pulled us over to the side of the road and got out with their torches to peruse the vehicles. The look on the faces when they saw inside was worth any trouble that was coming. They walked around both cars for several minutes trying to figure out who or what was what. They finally decided to arrest the drivers and leave the rest of the mess alone. Charley and I were carted off to Parramatta police station to be exhibited like freaks before the concerned constabulary.

The Parramatta police were amused and seemed grateful for the entertainment. We weren't drunk or belligerent and were happy to answer all of their questions. It was as if they had captured an alien space craft and were unsure of how to communicate with the crew. They asked us about punk and about what our parents thought. They inspected our clothes and marveled at our general weirdness. The final frontier had now been reached and the only remaining concern was our musical status. They wanted to know whether we were stars or had just come from the stars. One officer was convinced that all musicians were wealthy and asked us why we were driving what we were instead of travelling in limousines. The takings for our nights work were still in my jacket so I removed the plastic bags from my pockets and emptied the contents on the table. It was all small coins with the occasional dollar bill. We told them that it was a long way to the top. Everyone in the west was an AC/DC fan in those days so they laughed and thought that we were ok after all. They let us go without pressing charges. We left the station and were happy to find the punk caravan waiting for us outside. We all went back into town to celebrate!

After playing at the Royal Oak for over a year and trying hard to start some kind of punk scene in the West we decided to return to the city to play. We booked a gig at the Tropicana nightclub near the top of Oxford Street. This was one of the few gay clubs to actually turn straight in those days. We considered it to be a debut as we had been out west for so long that very few people in the city had heard us play. It did take around a year to get a good set written and for everyone to settle in so we felt that we were ready to rock n' roll. All the cool people turned up and you knew that they were cool because none of them danced. We got through the first set well and the response was very positive. There was a good buzz in the air and no one left early. We had a break half way through so we could work the room and socialize. Paul and Nick decided to go up to the Courthouse Hotel and buy a bottle of scotch instead. They then managed to drink the whole bottle before we got up for the second set. I never minded the band getting trashed on stage when it was the whole band. When it is only one or two members and the rest have to suffer along with the audience it can be a truly terrible experience. The gig went from great to ordinary very quickly and there was nothing that I could do about it. We went home in the van in a very bad mood with Tony telling us how we had blown it and that it was all over now. Although I hate to admit that Tony was ever right about anything, we all knew that it was true.

We did play on for some time but it was hard to find a new musical niche. We were still punks and although many people had reinvented themselves as mods or skins or rockers there was no way that I could sell out the last six years of my life in order to find some success in a new scene. We recorded a demo tape and took it to Lobby Lloyd's agency but got no response. Punk was still not popular amongst the rock n' roll fraternity and was still seen as an ideological threat to those who wanted to succeed. It was like the industry had become as conservative as the reactionaries that first attacked rock n' roll as the devil's music in the fifties. We ended up giving the four-track tape to a guy who put out a compilation album called Flowers from the Dustbin that had a picture of Jimmy on the cover looking like a goldfish. The songs that we chose were Black Cloud and Woe which were two titles that bore testament to our new outlook and the bleak mood that had descended on the Sydney punk scene.

The scene that we had help establish and had nursed like a baby was now walking on its own two feet. The Trade Union club was now a meeting place for young people from all over the city who were interested in an alternative scene. We would go there on most weekends and listen to Jay and the Brazilian Cockroaches play their unique mix of jazz with South American rhythms on the first floor while many different kinds of bands played upstairs. The Allniters and the Johnnies played there and pulled really good crowds. Ian Riland played there looking like Brian Ferry with his new band Sardine v. Overseas acts like B.B. King played there but even though our old punk pal Robbo the Yobbo ended up managing the joint no punk bands were ever allowed to play there. Punks were now just part of the furniture in the inner-city scene. We were like war veterans sitting unnoticed in a bar unless someone bothered to ask our story but then they would walk away bored anyway.

Our new-found anonymity was confirmed one night when I went to the toilet. A guy standing nearby starting muttering something under his breath and then walked out. I didn't care but he was waiting outside with two friends when I went to leave. They apparently thought that I was queer and started to insult me. We were blocked from the rest of the venue by a screen so no one else knew what was going on. We faced off for a while until the leader nodded to one of his minions and he came at me like an attack dog let off the leash. Vows of non-violence meant nothing in such situations and I felt that I was fighting for my life. We smashed through the door to the ladies and wrestled around for a while bashing each other's heads on the sink. Eventually we punched each other back outside again where we were finally interrupted by one of the bouncers. He dragged us apart but surprisingly didn't kick us out. I went back into the bar and walked over to a table where Jimmy was sitting. He told me that my assailants were friends of Freckles and that they were hardened criminals who would probably wait for me outside. I decided to front them in the bar while there was still some security around. I told them that I didn't want any more trouble. They laughed and said that was alright because they thought that I was a poofter but I did alright. One of them told me that they were armed robbers and that they were going to be famous. I said I would keep an eye on the news and asked them their names. The guy smiled at me with sneaky suspicion and said that he wasn't stupid so he couldn't tell me that. I didn't bother telling him how stupid that was.

Vellocette played our last three gigs in a row even though we didn't realise that they were our last gigs at the time. The first gig was our last gig at the Royal Oak and the pub stopped booking bands straight afterwards. We had completed our evangelical adventure and whether it was successful or not is not for me to say it was just good to get it done. This was a strange gig because it attracted a few people who were antithetical to our cause. There had been a number of scuffles during the night but nothing had broken out into a full-blown brawl. The other strange thing that happened was Spooner spitting on Jim's sister Bin. Bin and I had been seeing each other but spitting hadn't been seen in the scene for years. After the gig I was going to have a word with Spooner when I was distracted by a disruption in the venue. Some yobbo was bashing some young punk inside and It was a difficult situation because of my vow of non-violence. I had to step in and was lucky that the yobbo was really drunk and punching wild. He wasn't too big so I just kept blocking him and throwing him around. After a while he gave up and said he'd really like to meet me in the ring. This was weird because he couldn't really fight but we soon shook hands and left as friends. I went back to the car feeling confused and got even more confused when Spooner started to tease me about not bashing the yobbo to a bloody pulp. I forgot all about the spitting incident because all the way into town Spooner kept telling me that I had lost it. I still don't know what he thought that I had lost but whatever it was Spooner certainly didn't pick it up. By the time we got to his house I remembered the spitting incident. He got out of the car and went around the back to get his gear out. I knew that I couldn't bash him so I backed over him with the car instead.

The second gig was as support to the Kelpies at the Mosman Hotel. This was a huge gig and demonstrated how diverse and dynamic the music and cultural scene in Sydney had become. There were more straight people than there were punks. It was also the last time that some of the original punks from the Grand Hotel got to play together. Jimmy Bedhog from Black Runner fronted the Kelpies with Mark and Con from Suicide Squad playing in the band. Queen Anne's Revenge played first with all the original members of Chaos except that Captain Chaotic had been replaced by Crasti. Vellocette were the original Rejex without Richard. The Kelpies attracted a large following and had the best chance to be successful of any band from the scene. They even called themselves a post-punk band but were still infected by their punk past and the industry ignored them. Even though the scene had become an homogenous home to all kinds of kids there was still some friction between factions. Gary Skin came up to me in the toilets after the gig to tell me that there was going to be a fight between skins and punks. I asked him which side he was on and he got a bit confused. I told him that if he was going to start a fight, we could get it going right then and there. He ran from the toilets because he only liked to start fights that involved other people and because, like most skins, he couldn't fight at all on his own.

The last gig that we played was on our final road trip to Canberra. This involved a lot of new punk bands with Queen Anne's Revenge as headliners. The gig was held at a rehab centre outside of the city limits which was occupied by recovering drug addicts. There was also a fair share of mentally disabled people who wandered aimlessly around the venue without supervision. When we got to the front door of the hall it seemed as if the madness of the inmates had infected the punks as well. People were fighting and spewing and falling all over themselves all over the place. The cool calculated posturing and carefully constructed personas that had marked the early days of punk had been replaced by a chaotic drunken rabble. It was as if the havoc that we had wrought on society had finally come back to haunt us.

As we entered the hall a young punk tried to blindside me and Charley had to tackle him to the ground. This almost started an all-in brawl until Charley calmly got to his feet hugging the guy. He explained to everyone that they knew each other from out West and the violent expectation soon evaporated. We went and waited by the side of the stage until it was our turn to play. When we did it was the best musical experience of my musical experience. I had played before much bigger audiences and experienced accolades and encores, I had witnessed whole venues po going into a fanatical frenzy to our music, but here nothing happened at all. The fights and the chaos ceased and a strange calm descended over the venue. People did not dance but they did listen. We were literally calming the savage beast. This meant that by anyone's definition we were playing music and the music was good.

It was a wonderful experience and proved a most fitting and poetic way in which to end our musical careers. We walked from the stage straight into a guy named Donlan. He had been one of the surfies who had hassled Craig Jones in the library in high school all those years before. He now stood by the side of the stage with a large bag of pot and began rolling reefers. We all stood and celebrated our success. Donlan smoked while he told us how we had sold out and weren't really punk anymore. To be told what was punk by a pot smoking surfie was pretty funny. To be told this by a person who had mocked punk openly all those years ago was also hilarious. I couldn't be bothered arguing with him but stayed there as long as he was willing to roll the joints. The weirdness of the whole situation was wonderful and filled me with a feeling that I had truly come full circle.

Vellocette finally split up because of irreconcilable differences between the westy and the city factions even though most of the city faction came from the west. The irony of the situation was as pathetic as it was palpable. Charley wanted his friend Vern from the Section to join the band. It soon became apparent that they didn't want two guitarists but wanted Vern to replace Spooner. Apparently, they thought that Spooner was too gay for the group. Despite my differences with the Spooner Monster I was always a fiercely loyal friend and couldn't accommodate them. I tried my best at reconciliation but east is east and west is whatever. We had our final meeting at the Greystanes inn. This was the westie pub where I had had my first beer many moons ago. It was another sign that everything had gone full circle. I was the only one that wanted to keep going because I knew that this was the end of everything for everyone and none of us would get the chance to play in a truly original band ever again. It was like we were at a wake and I was insisting that the corpse would stand up but we all were out of miracles.

Bin and I got married at a Catholic church in Penrith at the end of 1982. It was the first time that the Punk congregation and a Catholic congregation would perform a ritual together. The church was filled with family and friends. Suits and ties clashed with coloured clothing which clashed all on its own. It was probably the strangest mix of people that the priest had ever seen. We went back to Bin's mothers house at Bargo for the reception. The same house where Danny Rumour and Jimmy Bedhog had begun their musical odyssey. All of our partners would fall pregnant the next year and the babies would be photographed playing together. I would say something about the circle of life but all these circles are making me dizzy.

We partied long into the night and punks and people crashed out all over the place. The following morning happy but extremely hung over we all lay around out the back of the house. Jimmy decided to show off for his city friends. He went up to the two horses who were busy minding their own business behind a fence. He picked the pure white Arab stallion and punched it in the head. He then jumped up on its back and raised his hands in the air in celebration. The horse bucked him straight back over its own head. Jimmy tumbled over and over before hitting the ground hard. The horse then walked slowly over to him and stomped once on his outstretched hand before walking away with a look of pure disdain. This would become metaphor for our future relationship. Jimmy would live the jumbled life of a junky for nearly forty years while I would watch from afar with my head in my hands. He would go head over heels to deny his healing while I would always believe in miracles. We drove back into town in his dads' truck with Bin and I in front and Jimmy laying in the back nursing his wounded pride. Sometimes you can travel in the same vehicle but be going in totally different directions, life can be funny like that!

AFTERWORD

If I could form a new social scene, I would call it the Necromantic Movement. It would be a celebration for all those who feel that their lifestyles have been vindicated by the advent of climate change. It would be the screaming acclamation that the rebels were right! The word Necromantic signifies the death of romance. Romance in relation to magic and nature and not in relation to personal emotional attachments. It would be marked by the colours purple, black and red signifying the sovereignty of anarchy. Anarchy is not the same thing as chaos. Anarchy is order derived from the collective will of the community instead of being imposed from above. Chaos is an agent of change and is always transitory because chaos by its nature cannot take control. The universe itself is an ordered state that came from chaos and chaos is coming whether we like it or not. If we are not willing to change then change will be forced upon us. If people had listened to the folk singers and beat poets protesting against the perils of pollution in the fifties or the sixties stoners telling us to tune in turn on and drop out we might not be in this position. Environmentalists are now called eco-terrorists. The punk protest was performance art that parodied the poisonous nature of this corrupt culture but even though we screamed in the seventies no one listened. No matter who you blame or what you believe you must admit that the rebels were right! It is not the punks or the poets or even the terrorists that are destroying the planet. It is the suited money men of mainstream society that are doing the real damage.

I'll finish with two more stories from the Bible so if you have any objections you had better blink. The first is the assertion by Jesus that 'None of those who cry out, 'Lord, Lord' will enter the kingdom of God but only the one who does the will of my father in heaven (Mat 7:21).' I do not pretend to know the will of God for anyone but I do not believe that it is Gods' will for us to condone or contribute to a culture that is destroying creation. Christianity was a radical religion that helped undermine the evil empire that was Rome. Now Christianity provides the foundation for the evil empire that is causing catastrophic climate change. Perhaps it is time for Christians to rediscover their radical roots and consider what is actually good rather than being minions of mammon.

The second biblical reference is the parable of The Wedding Banquet. The King calls all of his followers to the wedding feast of his son. The day of the feast comes and none of the invited guests turn up. The King sends his servants out again but they are insulted and ignored. The King gets angry and sends his soldiers out to destroy the invited guests. He then tells his servants to go out on the streets and gather together whatever total strangers they can find and invite them to the feast. They go out and invite anyone that they can find bad as well as good. When the King comes to the feast, he finds one man who is not properly dressed. He has him bound and thrown out into the street to wail and gnash his teeth (Mat 22: 1-14). People have received their invitations but they just aren't turning up. Perhaps you will have to be dressed as a punk or a hippy or in some other kind of radical robes in order to enter the pearly gates. Because sometimes what everyone thinks is the wrong thing can really be the right thing, the afterlife could be funny like that!

www.ingramcontent.com/pod-product-compliance
Lightning Source LLC
Chambersburg PA
CBHW041141110526
44590CB00027B/4085